# Second Sermons

# SECOND SERMONS

—Intimations of the Eternal—

Kenneth L. Vaux

Foreword by David M. Neff

WIPF & STOCK · Eugene, Oregon

SECOND SERMONS
Intimations of the Eternal

Copyright © 2015 Kenneth L. Vaux. All rights reserved. Except for brief quotations in critical publications or reviews, no part of this book may be reproduced in any manner without prior written permission from the publisher. Write: Permissions, Wipf and Stock Publishers, 199 W. 8th Ave., Suite 3, Eugene, OR 97401.

Wipf & Stock
An Imprint of Wipf and Stock Publishers
199 W. 8th Ave., Suite 3
Eugene, OR 97401

www.wipfandstock.com

ISBN 13: 978-1-4982-2289-1

Manufactured in the U.S.A.                              09/02/2015

# Contents

*Foreword by David M. Neff* | vii
*Acknowledgments* | xi
*Introduction* | xiii

1 Resurrection | 1
2 Heritage | 8
3 Bach I | 15
4 Bach II | 22
5 Mozart | 29
6 Gandhi | 35
7 Calvin | 45
8 Sonday | 48
9 Wesley | 55
10 Come Labor On | 71
11 Life Together | 77
12 Joy | 84
13 Sorrow | 89
14 Lion Power | 95
15 That Day/Wondrous Love | 111
16 Righteousness | 118
17 Reconciliation | 123
18 True Man | 130
19 True God | 139
Conclusion and Appraisal | 143

*Bibliography* | 145

# Foreword

I.

SECOND PRESBYTERIAN CHURCH OF Chicago has historically been considered an establishment church built by the affluent movers and shakers of the city of Chicago. Chartered in 1842, the congregation lived out its mission in two buildings downtown before building the current structure in 1874. In 1900, the church suffered a fire that devastated the interior of the sanctuary. Local architect and church member Howard Van Doren Shaw redesigned the entire sanctuary. His friend, noted artist Frederic Clay Bartlett, created the murals with other craftsmen executing the wood carvings, plaster panels, and other decorative details. The resulting Arts and Crafts style space has come to be recognized as a national treasure of art and artistry. With 175 angels and nine glorious Tiffany stained glass windows adorning the sanctuary, the church has occupied a prominent place in the history of Chicago's great families and within the larger history of Chicago. Named a National Historic Landmark in 2013—the only church in the city of Chicago to be designated—the congregation offers a traditional Protestant worship on Sunday mornings, with incredible organ music and a professional quartet.

Entering the sanctuary, the worshiper sees a centrally located pulpit, elevated on the dais. Above the ornately carved woodwork, elaborate brass organ screen, and hanging lamps, the Tree of Life mural invites one to contemplate and embrace the majesty of God the Creator, to experience the harmonies and goodness of created life. A starry ordered universe is accessible to faith, with angels ever-trumpeting and praising God. At the conclusion of worship, after the choral benediction and postlude, as one turns to leave the sanctuary, the worshiper's gaze looks upward to see the Five Scourges of Christ from Holy Week (the cord of ropes, the whip, the chains, the cross, the nails and stakes, and crown of thorns). Above them is the great Ascension window: Christ being raised victorious over suffering and sin, tragedy and evil. The resurrection and ascension reveal that his righteous life and faithful witness are vindicated and crowned by the resurrection of glory. Everything we suffer will be taken up into the greater triumph of the love of God.

But where is the Holy Spirit represented in this architectural masterpiece? Where is the *Pneuma Hagia*, the *Spiritu Sanctu* as designed within this well-designed theological and liturgical space? I often think about this and reflect on it as I sit in the sanctuary for meditation and prayer, which is the best part of my job as pastor.

II.

When the Reverend Dr. Kenneth Vaux served as the interim pastor here during 1991 and 1992, this once-thriving congregation was in decline. As the South Loop of Chicago became abandoned warehouses and boarded-up buildings, members moved out of the city to the suburbs. As the neighborhood around the church changed to a place that was dark and scary at night, the mission changed. With fewer members and resources, mission became difficult.

Nearly twenty-five years later, the congregation still struggles to find its identity and its mission. The South Loop has become the fastest-growing residential neighborhood in Chicago. High-rise condominiums, upscale townhomes, and pricy apartments are being developed weekly. The creation of an Entertainment District, a new Green Line El stop, and expansion of McCormick Place will bring in more people to live and work. While there are mixed and low-income apartment buildings within blocks of the church, the congregation has struggled to reach out and embrace a new constituency, often falling back on its impressive traditions. Within the past few years, many residents have expressed the thought that the church has been closed or has become a museum.

Second Presbyterian Church is in the midst of a time of vibrant revivification and resurrection. Its members and friends are engaged in becoming more of a presence in the community. Always warm in its welcome, the church is expanding its hospitality and increasing both religious and

# Foreword

non-religious programming to meet the needs of high-rise dwellers around us. In reaching out, the congregation is being renewed spiritually, as we extend ourselves to get to know our community and try more thoughtfully to serve in ministry to the needs of those around us.

In the past ten years, we have grown into a lively multicultural congregation. Because the church receives people from every walk of life, those who enter its doors want a lively faith—a real faith that will help them navigate the challenges of life.

## III.

Ken Vaux's preaching represents "the church of the future" (Hans Kung). His sermons in this collection represent a faith that is real and relevant. Speaking to both head and heart, his words offer hope to the young and the elderly, to all who seek a connection between the life of the church and the life of the world. The church exists as an intellectual community. Its ideas span the history of time even before the church existed. The treasures of his theology speak of a real dialogue between Christ and culture, the supreme relevance of religion to every aspect of society. His sermons speak of keeping the Word of God before us, as we seek to be faithful in living and responsible to the world around us. They speak of a real God who calls us to live a demanding life, then offers us grace through the mediation of a community of nurture and support.

At the same time, the church is also an artistic community that celebrates the holy gifts of music, dance, theater, art, and architecture—passed down through time immemorial—in the context of worship. The church is at its best when "every instrument is tuned for praise" (Wren) and uses all the arts to illuminate God the Great Artist.

Finally, the church is a place of engagement and activism. In Professor Vaux's sermons, you will hear a passion for the world around us, and an emphasis on the church as an agent for justice locally and peace globally. The church is never called to institutional maintenance, but to lose its life for the world for which Christ gave his life. This "holy worldliness" (Bonhoeffer) makes these sermons gifts to the church and to seekers of every age.

Perhaps there is no other way to symbolize the invisible yet palpable Holy Spirit other than through the people who gather each week for worship and praise, then scatter into the world after study and fellowship to

## Foreword

embody the Word. Ken Vaux points us to that Spirit which is holy, ever-present in the church, calling us ever to life made new through faith.

Reverend Dr. David M. Neff
Second Presbyterian Church

# Acknowledgments

THANKS TO EDITORS DAVID Jones (Evanston) and the excellent Wipf & Stock team: Matthew Wimer, Justin Haskill, and Ian Creeger for good work on a very difficult project. Thanks also to Mary Kay Duff for a subvention gift honoring her father, John Duff, of Watseka, Illinois. Thanks for another subvention from Coach Ron Adams (Golden State Warriors) and his wife, Leah. As always, the support of Sara Anson Vaux, our children and grandchildren has been indispensible.

K. V.

# Introduction

As the July sun—warm and moist—rises over Lake Michigan, my awakening thoughts run to the glorious golden tones of the Tiffany Ascension window that shimmer at this hour through the east façade of Second Presbyterian Church on Michigan and 18th on the south end of the "Magnificent Mile." This church has been the south city scene of my ministry in various roles for the last twenty years.

On this morning I draw myself up to my Grammy Shoup's writing table facing into the south and east picture window of the study where that same sun also rises.

"Veda" was a learned and literate lady, abandoned by her father as a child, yet remaining an inimitable presence. When she married "Pap," Lester Shoup, ninety years ago, they ordered this desk from the Sears Catalogue—$12—I believe. It was delivered to her little house on the banks of the Scrubgrass Creek. Here she would sit each night before she retired, writing diary notes and letters with her flowing and elegant hand. In one entry made when I was a youth living in New York in 1950, she penned these words on this day, July 10:

> ... Dad pumped (Quaker State oil fields) until 12
> Bee and Janie (my then 12 year-old cousin) came, helped clean up house
> Pap and Janie got 2 chickens ready for Bee.

Today, as I write at her desk, world events are more momentous than in those post-war years of the Truman presidency. Last night Israel fired 320 rockets into a frantically frustrated Gaza—killing a family of eight in their home and five persons in a bar watching the World Cup as Argentina narrowly beat Holland. Meanwhile President Obama was in Dallas, Texas, encouraging "faith-based organizations" to help with the humanitarian crisis

# Introduction

of tens of thousands of children fleeing violence-ridden Central America to seek refuge in this nation that had always—until now—beckoned the world to "send me your tired masses—yearning to breathe free"—UNTIL NOW! By week's end Israel would have invaded Gaza and a Malaysian Air 777 would have been shot down on the Russia/ Ukraine border killing 290 persons.

In some mysterious way common things and cataclysmic events remain strangely similar. My own vehicle to interpret personal, historical, and theological events has been the written memoir structured on some theme. The undergirding substance in this diary—in which I will interpolate (with my Barthian penchant) notes about Bible truth, common life, and world news—will be a series of sermons which I offered as interim minister at Second Presbyterian twenty years ago.

Preacherships are peculiarly Protestant institutions established around the time of Zwingli, Luther, and Calvin in the regions of Switzerland, Germany, and France. These were delivered to establish the demands of an educated and animated laity for learned biblical exposition to accompany liturgy and eucharist in order to sustain the congregation's ministries in the world.

This present preachership was inspired by the master Lake Poet William Wordsworth who used the phrase, "Intimations of the Eternal." It offers nineteen sermons on the overarching theme: "Sacraments—Intimations of the Eternal in our Common Life." Here you will find the particular messages I shared with the congregation in President Lincoln's family church in 1991–1992. Some were written earlier, others later. I also will add some new sermons from my present service in the church as a parish associate along with interpretive comments on the history and current events of the church.

I will now share with you a look at this year of preaching sometimes with the whole message, other times with a brief summary. Wordsworth's famous poem contains the phrase "The child is the father of the man; / and I wish my days to be / bound . . . by natural piety."[1]

This "natural piety" is the leitmotif of the enclosed *Second Sermons* along with their hermeneutical notes.

Wordsworth found in all nature and experience—calm and violent, fortunate and misfortunate, the "intimation" or hint of the divine and the eternal.

---

1. Wordsworth, "Ode: Intimations of Immortality from *Recollections of Early Childhood*." http://www.poetryfoundation.org/poem/174805

## Introduction

"The babe leaps up in his mother's arm . . . I hear with joy . . . A tree and field speak of something that is gone . . . the pansy that is at my feet doth the same tale repeat . . . Where is fled the visionary gleam . . . Trailing clouds of glory do we come from God, who is our home."[2]

Comments: Life with all joy and sorrow is passing. It is ephemeral. All tokens of our experience speak of a sublime beyond. The cascade of themes which the sermon series spanned were such reminders, hints—sacraments or icons—glimpsing (or trailing) eternity.

2. Ibid.

# 1

# Resurrection[1]

The blank misgivings of a creature
Our noisy years seem moments on the being of the eternal silence...[2]

At last they heard Aslan's voice:—"You can all come back," he said. "I have settled the matter [of eternal justice and recompense]. She [the wicked witch to whom has been yielded momentarily the death of the creator lion] has renounced the claim on your brother's blood."

The great lion faces down the forces of evil and death, submitting his great and good life even unto death and is raised from the dead.[3]

## MEDITATION ON ACTS 3 (PHILLIPS TRANSLATION)[4]

One afternoon Peter and John were on their way to the temple for the three o'clock hour of prayer. A man who had been lame from

---

1. Preached at Second Presbyterian Church, Chicago—Eastertide, 1993
2. Wordsworth, "Ode: Intimations of Immortality,."
3. Lewis, *The Lion, the Witch*, 158.
4. This first sermon went right to the heart of my own faith position and to the crux of the sacred reality—death, resurrection, and healing.

> birth was being carried along in the crowd, for it was the daily practice to put him down at what was known as the "Beautiful Gate of the Temple," so that he could beg from the people as they went in. As this man saw Peter and John just about to enter, he asked them to give him something. Peter looked intently at the man and so did John. Then Peter said, "Look straight at us!" The man looked at them expectantly, hoping that they would give him something.

"If you are expecting silver or gold," Peter said to him, "I have neither, but what I have I will certainly give you. In the name of Jesus Christ of Nazareth, walk!"

Then he took him by the right hand and helped him up. At once his feet and ankle bones were strengthened, and he positively jumped to his feet, stood, and then walked about, leaping and praising God. Everyone noticed him as he walked and praised God and recognized him as the same beggar who used to sit at the beautiful gate, and they were all overcome with wonder and sheer astonishment at what had happened to him. Then while the man himself still clung to Peter and John, all the people in their excitement ran together and crowded round them in Solomon's Porch. When Peter saw this he spoke to the crowd.

> "Men of Israel, why are you so surprised at this, and why are you staring at us as though we had made this man walk through some power or piety of our own? It is the God of Abraham and Isaac and Jacob, the God of our fathers, who had done this thing to honor his servant Jesus—the man whom you betrayed and denied in the presence of Pilate, even when he had decided to let him go. But you disowned the holy and righteous one, and begged to be granted instead a man who was a murderer! You killed the prince of life, but God raised him from the dead—a fact of which we are eyewitnesses."

My thesis of this *lectur* (Calvin's French word for sermon) is this: Resurrection degenerates into shallow Easter Bunny fantasy when disjoined from healing, just as healing collapses to mere juvenation apart from resurrection. As C. S. Lewis reminded the world in the book *Miracles*, everything, including all miracles and healings, hinges on this grand miracle—the resurrection of Jesus Christ.

It was probably at the East Gate of the temple where they laid him. Nicanor it was called, the majestic gate called "Beautiful." It was here that the small plateau of Mt. Jerusalem falls off sharply. Here the road winds down into the Kedron Valley then meanders south toward Bethlehem. Across the valley are ancient, gnarled olive trees that have stood since Jesus anguished there and give the mount its name. The garden at the base is called Gethsemane. You can walk around that foot path wrapping the south side of olive mountain leading to *Bethani* and *Bethphage.*

As the lame man lay there, he could survey the panorama. King David—that irascible, beloved one—often processed through that gate. One *Jeshua,* who was accused of posing as "King of the Jews," rode up through that gate some weeks before, on a donkey no less, in one of the many small demonstrations that always enlivened Passover. But David and Jesus—that history was not this invalid's story. He knew of David, and we might surmise that he had heard of Jesus. But one lame from birth cannot follow, nor could he mingle to hear the marketplace gossip. But he may have sensed something. Those who lose some facilities often develop others of heightened sensitivity. Perhaps he felt the vibrations and tremors that only the mystic can feel; perceptions tell you that something is happening, history is changing. Perhaps he intuited that something new was being unleashed into human life.

Most likely the wretch came simply for a handout. Waifs of all kinds have always gathered at the beautiful gates of our temples. They are often seen at our church door or in our parking lot. Too frequently, we have turned them away. How tragic it is that the church has forfeited the arm of charity to the state in modern history. The churches in the cities are often barred and locked against the poor. The poor of the earth will continue to camp at our beautiful gate because the state can only dispense assistance. It cannot love.

The crippled man lay there pleading in the afternoon sun as the crowd scurried into the temple. Peter and John, sons of the resurrection, were among the synagogue crowd going to Tephilim, the Jewish service of prayer. The departure of the church from the synagogue and the synagogue from the church is another tragic event. But that's another story.

The crippled man reached out for Peter and John. The confrontation was intense. It recalled the soul-searching gaze of Jesus into the eyes of Peter at Caserea Phillipi and again on the porch of betrayal. "Look at us," they commanded. "I have no silver or gold. But I give you what I have. In the name of Jesus Christ of Nazareth, WALK!"

Regrettably, we may ask if the church has ever again been so materially poor yet so spiritually rich as on that afternoon. Since then, we are more like the rich young ruler saying to Jesus, "I have followed all the laws from my youth," and Jesus still commands: "Sell all you have and give to the poor."

Jesus still commands and commends Warren Buffett to ask his fellow million- and billionaires to "sell all they have and give to the poor." He still commands and commends the poor widow to give her last mite. But above all this supererogatory talk, he simply asks us all to give what we have. In his name, the lame may walk, the poor find sufficiency, the blind see, the hungry be fed, the homeless be sheltered, the dead be raised. Our gifts and his commands then, now, and forever bring resurrection and life. His power is become our ministry.

Surely it is Luke the physician who makes this recollection: "He took him by the right hand and raised him up; and immediately his feet and ankles were made strong." This is a physician and icon-maker writing. The passage is couched in diagnostic and therapeutic language. It is envisioned by a Greek mystical artist. You can see it and touch it. It is not the idealized spirituality of a "Moonie" or a Mary Baker Eddy healer. It is down to earth, concrete, believable—and like it or not— it is instructive to us.

"Men of Israel why do you wonder at this?" "Why do you stare at us as though our own power or piety made him whole." The picture almost breathes other words of Jesus: "This afflicted one was not born thusly to punish him or his father—it was that the Father God might be glorified." Peter continues in that vein—"Jesus, the author of life, Son of Abraham, whom you delivered and denied and killed whom God raised from the dead." His power released this healing on this man through his faith and your touch "making him whole before your very eyes."

Healing empowered by resurrection—the New Testament's way of talking about the most powerful reality in human life. Resurrection and healing are two complementary and synergic notions that forever astonish and baffle the human mind. Held together they make terrible and believable sense. Severed, they bring chaos to the world. Resurrection degenerates into Easter Bunny fantasy when disjoined from healing, just as healing collapses into mere juvenation when divorced from resurrection. Together they constitute the abundance of life (John 20:31). Paul Tillich found "The Courage to Be" in the conjunction of resurrection and healing. A glance at the sad parade of faith healers who more often destroy faith than restore health, or the array of mechanistic practicioners who impose their iatrogenic diseases, gives evidence of the tragic yield of the separation.

## Resurrection

Resurrection and healing each entail the other. "Resurrection is verified," wrote William Stringfellow, "where strife against the demonic thrives."[5] What an excellent description of the parade of healings in Peter's gospel as composed by Mark.

Resurrection is a universal symbol. It comes from and belongs to everyone, everywhere. It appears in primitive religion. Think of Frazier's *Golden Bough* with the corn gods and the Canaanite and Sumerian fertility gods. The Jews believed in resurrection for a long time—especially in the prophetic and apocalyptic periods. The appearance of Christ as Jesus in the world brings resurrection home to everyone. Resurrection is life beyond death. Healing is life—always on the verge of brokenness—being made whole. One can be healed even as he is sick and dying. Kierkegaard spoke of sickness and "Sickness unto Death." Lazarus was dead as a doornail yet his sickness was not unto death. Commenting on this narrative Kierkegaard—indeed most existentialism, speaks of "living death." Life in Sartre and Kafka can be the cocoon, the apartment with "no exit." Death can be the open door to glorious life.

Resurrection and healing blend and intermingle. The Greek word "soteria" means healing and salvation. Dr. Luke elsewhere refers to the fishermen mending their nets as soteria. In Latin we have words salvus, salve, salvation, salut—health. In the Germanic tongue it is Heil and Heilig—Holy—hale. Important distinctions exist between the Hellenic doctrine of "immortality of the soul" and the Hebraic doctrine of "resurrection of the body." Christians as Jews believe in new being, new heaven, new earth. In faith and hope there is a kind of protest—of forward inclination. "Those who hope in Christ," writes Jürgen Moltmann, "cannot put up with reality as it is . . . They chafe under it, resist it, for the goad of the unfulfilled future stabs inexorably into every unfulfilled present."[6]

The opposite is also true. Destruction and disease, sin and sickness are part of the syndrome of finitude—the drive towards death. But death precedes life in nearly every case. There is death in the miracle of human conception and birth. The seed must die to give life. Conserving old shells and wineskins makes no sense when reality is thus understood. Erich Fromm has shown how two human impulses and compulsions drive through existence with relentless force. We are biophilic or necrophilic—life loving or death loving—often a mingled dialectic of the two. We are open to the

---

5. Stringfellow, *Public and Private Faith*.
6. Moltmann, *Theology of Hope*, 10.

future or closed. We yearn for the future or we cling to the past, the womb. The biophile in us is fascinated with life, persons, relationships—with love. The necrophile within us is fascinated with things, cars, TV, laws and order, gadgets, violence and destruction. The future of life on earth will be decided by the human answer to this dichotomy.

The task of the Christian in the world, indeed the meaning of being human in the world, is to be a healer, to be a savior as Paul Tillich has said. It is to be an agent of resurrection and reconciliation. This is what our life and our common life is about. Healing entails inner and outer openness.[7]

## HEALING IS AN INWARD OPENNESS.

Disease is always an inner restriction, a turning inward. The schizophrenic and autistic is afraid to look you in the eye for fear you will see him. The paranoiac retreats from the world that is closing in on him. Uncle Sam in the tax collector had his hand in your pocket. Business colleagues are stepping on you in order to get ahead. In the communistic, socialist conspiracy everything around you is being infected. Luther called sin and sickness curator in se—curved in on oneself. Freud saw in patients an ego-centricity, a self-absorbtion, internalized stress, suppression of feeling. Narcissism is navel gazing, the individualization of nationalism—leading to illness and thwarting wellness in the person and community.

By contrast, Spirit-Life, resurrection life is expansive—open to the world and the new. Beyond psychedelia and halluciogenia this kind of life awareness is full and deep. It is vibrant and free. Integrity—wholesome abundance—is the gift of healing and resurrection. This mood integrates the organic dimension of life into the whole without collapsing into materialism. Only children of the resurrection are free to love life, love the earth as Nietzsche and Kazantzakis have said. Only she can love the body and dance in the temple as this lame one did. Resurrection life is multidimensional, which saves one from becoming one-dimensional (cf. *One Dimensional Man*). It is Herbert Marcuse who says that "technological man" is being pressed into this one dimension. Progress is rationalized so that human life is subverted into the reproductive cycle. The sick society can only become the sane society if thing-fascination can be transformed into life-fascination.

---

7. See Tillich, *Courage to Be*.

# Resurrection

It is necrophilia—die in the tomb, anti-resurrection, that allows our national and local infrastructures to rot away and die while we bomb to smithereens the ancient cities of Arabia and the Middle East through invasions and occupations. It is necrophilia that allows Rodney King or Michael Brown to be killed by the police or a bewildered woman on the freeway to be thrown to the ground and beaten. The law has become the vehicle of brutality.

## HEALING IS ALSO OUTWARD OPENNESS.

Peter had something that could not be kept down. Stones can be collected and vegetables pickled. But the important things in life cannot be kept. Try to keep love and watch it turn to lust. Try to keep peace to yourself and watch it turn into passivity. Try to keep money and watch it turn into mammon. Try to keep Christ and you become a bigot. Christ and his resurrection power will be released into the world. Peter and John shared what they had. It was all that they had. It was enough. We are given in service to the world. We are waiters waiting to give what God is doing in the world. We anticipate and welcome the new humanity which is being ushered into the creation. This renevatio—this new creation—new heaven and earth is impending. It is breaking forth.

In conclusion, we must speak of how we can enter into healing and resurrection. Life in this order is realized in suffering. Paul captures his life's journey: "That I may know him and the power of his resurrection, and may share his sufferings, becoming like him in his death, that if possible I may attain the resurrection of the dead" (Phil 3: 10–11). In one of his last letters from prison, Dietrich Bonhoeffer expressed it this way: "It is only by living completely in this world that one learns to believe. One must abandon every attempt to make something of oneself, whether it be a saint, a sinner, a church man, a righteous man or an unrighteous man, a sick or healthy one. This is what I mean by worldliness—taking one's life in stride, with all its duties and problems, its successes and failures, its experiences and helplessness. It is in such a life that we throw ourselves utterly into the arms of God and participate in his sufferings in the world and watch with Christ in Gethsemane."[8]

---

8. Comments: As Bonhoeffer wrote in the remarkable "this worldly" writings in his sojourn in Spain entitled *No Rusty Swords*, true life is surrender into the "sufferings of God."

# 2

# Heritage[1]

CHICAGO 1992—LIKE 1942 OR 1892 or 1842, for that matter—seems to be the best of times; or is it the worst of times?

Chicago 1992:

The roof of an underground tunnel collapses spilling millions of gallons of river water into the basements of Chicago's great buildings causing perhaps $1 billion in damage and losses.

The Bulls and Blackhawks are still in the running for world championships.

While at old Wrigley, the Cubs are nestled customarily near the bottom, and at new Comiskey the Sox are poised, as expected, near the top.

The city with broad shoulders dismantles huts for the homeless under the Halsted tracks, as it plans for a third airport, a gambling casino, and property-tax caps.

---

This first sermon ends with the beginning and begins with the end. The foundational intimation of eternity in secularity is seen when death becomes life and life, death. All other intimations will follow in this wake. Ancient wisdom remarked—"The King is dead, the dead is arisen, Long live the King."

1. Sermon: "Heritage and Hope," Second Presbyterian Church, Chicago on the occasion of its 150th anniversary, May 31, 1992. Scriptures: Ps 127:1–2; Matt 16:13–18; Heb 3:1–6. Our second Second Sermon is quite different from the first intimation on "Resurrection." Rather than a theological meditation on resurrection and healing this one is occasioned by an event of historical commemoration where memory is invoked to inspire in the congregation renewed dedication and hope.

## Heritage

And here on the South Side—in the shadow of this dazzling and desperate megalopolis—a company of Christians gathers and dares to confess Christ before the city and resolves to live in renewed faith and hope into the second half of its second century.

Our predecessors in these pews 50, 100, 150 years ago would be shocked and surprised to see Chicago today. They'd be shocked at the casino, racetrack, and riverboat gambling—they'd be horrified at Lotto's blasphemous advertising slogan—"the odds be with you." They were more candid about the psychology of temptation and piety than we are in our "live and let live" age.

But, I think, they'd be pleased to see us here today . . . Afro, Asian, and Euro Americans—young and old, rich and poor. We have achieved a diversity that Presbyterians have always believed in and hoped for, but seldom achieved. That congregation that more than a century ago applauded the abolitionist and contributed to the underground railroad to aid escaping slaves—applauds us today from the clouds. They gathered here in front of the church under the Ascension Window and grieved with President Lincoln's widow and son, members of this congregation.

A goodly heritage . . . a godly hope. Our foundation and building is secure—our future is sure and promising, no misplaced piling or leaks over our subterranean tunnels. Christ has cleared the pits and entered paradise. Built on this bedrock we seek today to renew a good confession. Our Scriptures ground us in the truth about confession and congregation.

Psalm 89 is a kingly psalm. Is the record of a commemoration service such as the one we celebrate today. The people recall God's mighty acts of deliverance and covenant.

They pledge renewed faithfulness and righteousness.

I will sing thy steadfast love, O Lord, forever. With my mouth I will proclaim thy faithfulness to all generations. Righteousness and justice are the foundation of thy throne. Steadfast love and faithfulness go before thee. Blessed are the people who know the festal shout, who walk in the light of thy countenance and who shout and jump as the song and dance goes—our sister act and our brother act. "The church with Psalm must shout," wrote George Herbert, "no door can keep them out. Let all the world in every corner sing—my God and King."

Confession and profession: faithfulness is saying and doing good word, God Word.

Psalm 127 is a warning:

Unless the Lord builds the house—they labor in vain who build it. Activity, even hyperactivity, without Word, is quixotic—beating at the wind. How often the church has become frenetic in self-occupation and self aggrandizement while a world hungry for Gospel and help goes wanting. "But didn't we cry Lord—Lord didn't we sing the right thing." "He who does my father's will; will enter the Kingdom." Words without love and work are noisy gongs or clanging cymbals (1 Cor 13).

The faith we have inherited and share with our Hebrew forbearers is that given us at the opening of the Bible. God willed and created, and it was good.

## CONFESSION. INTENTION. ACTION.

When we move to the New Covenant, the New Testament, the New Confession, the note is the same. In the beginning was the Word, and the word didn't just sit there; the word became flesh. Intention, action, word, will, work. Truth is in order to goodness, contends all noble religion. It is the keystone of our book of order, "By their fruit, ye shall know them."

Take Peter's confession: there is generality and specificity in all confession. Who do men say that the son of man is? That's the question to the philosopher? To the politician? What in general is your worldview? What are your family values? Waiting for Perot, perhaps we say, "I have principles but no programs." But who do you say that I am?

Now this hits home. You know we are Rocky two? We mark today the glorious threshold of summer; our children are now graduating or commencing from nursery and grade school, from high school and college, from graduate, professional or trade school. For many, it is a moment of introspection, confession and profession. In houses of worship, it is a time of *mishpatim* and confirmation. It is a time for many of our sons and daughters to stand up, take a deep breath, not look back and say to the world: "This is who I am. This is who I want to be. I want this loyalty to mark my life." Just saying the words in front of other people seems to tie it down. We become what we confess. We damn or bless ourselves with what we believe in our heart and confess with our mouth. Word is conformation.

Autonomically, we say the creed, the Lord's prayer, even the Lord's supper. We utter our eternal benefit: Jesus is Lord! The words make it come true. Unless we were "Big Tuna" Accardo, everyone here has been called forward at some time to make confession.

- Will you say a word to this young person?
- Will you teach this class?
- Will you pray at our dinner?
- Will you lead worship?

Confession is one of the most awesome phenomena of the human spirit: it changes us. And like Peter we're on the spot and we think it and we say it and suddenly, perhaps even to our own surprise, it is so. "You are the Christ. The son of the living God" and as we say it, it is confirmed within us and we are conformed to it. We become Rocky too! You are Petros and on this rock (petra) I will build my church and the gates of hell shall not prevail against it.

Confession of life is always made against threat and adversity, against the powers of death. There is an ominous stillness and secrecy in this scene in Matthew. He charged them strictly to tell no one that he was the Christ. The trek to Calvary had begun. Jesus, says the Epistle to the Hebrews, is the high priest of our confession. He is the sacrifice that seals our pronounced loyalty in life and death.

Dietrich Bonhoeffer, who wrote a commentary on Matthew called *The Cost of Discipleship*, said that "when Christ calls a person, he bids 'him come and die.'" Martyrdom was in the air when our parents of the Heidelberg confession asked and answered: "Who is your only hope in life and death? My only hope in life and death is my faithful Savior Jesus Christ."

Anticipation of cross-like Nazi gallows pierced the sky for his friend Bonhoeffer when Karl Barth wrote the Barmen Declaration. It was the sign of the confessing church of Germany and now has an honored place in our *Book of Confessions*. We confess the truth that Christ, not the state, not the church, is Lord.

From these scriptures and sacred text let us consider in conclusion three aspects of a good confession: these are qualities of faith, which honor our heritage and enliven our hope:

1. We make our confession before the demonic and death.

2. Before a disbelieving world and,

3. Before the generations.

"Where Christ erechteth His Church," wrote Richard Bancroft in 1600, "the devil in the same churchyard will have his chapel. But the yawning gates of death and hell shall not prevail against the rock of a Christ confession."[2]

In the wake of Memorial Day this week, as the caverns of violent death opened again in Sarajevo, in the Gaza Strip, in Haiti, WFMT played Benjamin Britten's "War Requiem." This magnificent oratorio was composed for the rededication of Coventry Cathedral. When you visit Coventry you still see the shell of the old cathedral destroyed by Nazi bombs. The 1940s, like the 1990s, were times when the demonic was ever present. Now in the power of Coventry's confession a new stark and dramatic sanctuary has risen from the rubble.

Like the Kaiser Wilhelm Confessing Church in Berlin, also constructed next to the shell of its bombed out predecessor, the Confessing Church rises toward eternal life amid the rubble of human violence and death. We confess against the dread of death.

She lay dying with cancer, a young mother, sheer and bitter tragedy. Leaving young children behind and a husband who loved her dearly. The pain, the nausea, the indignity; this was the end, it's over—no, not quite. Her last words: "I am baptized, Christ is my Lord! I will lay me down in peace for thou Lord makest me dwell in safety." With his own blood he bought her, and for her life he died. The winter is past. The pain is over.

Our confession is made before the demonic and death. It is also made before a disbelieving world. God seems to have abandoned twentieth century humanity to its folly. We can grow genetically engineered super tomatoes, but not citizens. We can jimmy a satellite back secure onto the shuttle *Endeavor* in deep space yet we can't secure and heal a sector of Los Angeles. The world is caught up and condemned in its pretense and its obliviousness to need and injustice. A suburban church would not let its kids come to Comiskey Park a few weeks ago. It feared racial and gang violence.

A North Shore Presbyterian spoke for thousands recently when he said: "No more taxes, no more AIDS, no more unwed mothers, no more dying—no more city."

The city can be Jacques Ellul's house of dereliction—but Harry Nilsson was right and that North Shore geek wrong. "I guess the Lord must be in New York City."

"This is where God is," pleads Martin Scorcese in *Mean Streets*. Some would say of us what Jonathan Swift said of St. Anne's, Dublin: "A beggarly people; a church without a steeple."

---

2. Bancroft, *Sermon on Christ*, n.p.

# Heritage

But God has placed our lives and our church, even with its blown-down steeple, here in the city, and we bless you from north, south, and west, who have come to show solidarity with us. The world betrays its unbelief by its poverty of heart and soul.

Finally, our confession is made from generation to generation. We pause today with thanksgiving for 150 years into a remarkable heritage. We thank those women and men, those youth and children; all who made a good confession, who kept the faith, who built the church, who came back from fire and sword, who made the coffee, spread the table, planted the tulips, ran the rummage sales, prepared the meals, tutored the children, comforted the bereaved, visited the sick, welcomed the visitor, invited the friend, offered the handouts—all in the name of the good confession, Jesus is Lord. In every gesture of care:

- they insured that the Gospel was sounded in word and music,
- that the faith and life was conveyed in dedicated teaching,
- that pastoral care was provided,
- that authentic Christian behavior was exemplified.

We also pledge our faith to generations to come. To our children and the children of this city, and to the persons who are making their lives in our part of the city: the young adults, the singles, the mothers and children, those struggling to make it through the day, those struggling to make a living. We pledge ourselves to renew this city; to renovate its buildings, to enhance its beauty, to make our streets smart and safe, to strengthen family and community, to provide love and care in the neighborhood, to sustain a sense of prayer for all people where God can be known, worshiped and served, in sum, to seek a lovely and sustainable world for generations to come.

And our most solemn and sacred trust is to be true to Christ and to Christ's future. Let us pledge with all the strength within us to present him as Lord to future generations, and to that end we will teach and pray, worship and sing, reach out and love, work and march, all to a good confession. "Lord, knowing that unless you build the house we who build it labor in vain. Unless you watch over the city, we stay awake in vain." We would be building now those temples still undone! Amen.

Comments: This sermon was assisted by Mary Morrison, the daughter of a member of Second Pres.—Bonnie Wilke—before Mary herself prepared to become a Presbyterian pastor. (Mary died unexpectedly on

November 25, 2014.) The service and sermon was an event which showed the strengths and flaws of my own preaching, the commitment to a church in the city and the elegance of Princeton, Fourth Pres., Chicago style with all too much of that formalism, politicization, and intellectual arrogance of that same heritage. Across the years the people at Second helped to mold this professor/pastor to be one more suitable to the pulpit.

# 3

# Bach I[1]

*Nicht Bach, Meer sollte er heissen* [He should not be called a brook but the ocean]

—Ludwig van Beethoven

I expressed it to myself as if the eternal harmony were communing with itself, as might have happened in God's bosom shortly before the creation of the world. It was thus that my inner depths were stirred and I seemed neither to possess or need ears, still less eyes, or any other sense

—Johann Wolfgang Von Goethe (after hearing Schütz playing Bach's *Well-Tempered Clavier*)

In this season of the year Bach's genius again overwhelms us. Not only in the realms of Lutheranism but throughout the Christian world and indeed the interreligious and secular world. Wintertide and Christmastide belongs to J. S. Bach for all time. The *Magnificat* was written for the Christmas eve-

---

1. This sermon was preached at Second Pres. in the spring of 1991. Earlier versions were presented at First Unitarian and University Presbyterian in Houston, Texas, over the Christmas week in December of 1972.

ning service of 1723—Bach's first *Weinachtszeit* in Leipzig. The *Mass in B Minor* and *The Christmas Oratorio* and the tunes "Jesu Meine Freude" and "Jesu, Joy of Man's Desiring" also come to mind.

Music is a universal intimation in the sense understood first by Pythagoras who grouped it with mathematics and spiritual transcendence as sensors of truth and divinity. Bach and Mozart especially fathom these natural and supernal wellsprings.

As a cultural critic and public theologian, I am well aware that Christmas is an American and Northern European festival now thoroughly corrupted by Western materialism and shopping until dropping—rituals now made so much worse by the enduring and seemingly unremovable ethical stigmata and stain of gnawing poverty throughout both worlds of rich and poor. Song, however, gladdens the heart of all people and Bach's song gives the whole world reason to rejoice and hope. The New England pastor—Phillips Brooks—who wrote "O Little Town of Bethlehem" from his parish in the snow bedecked hills—rightly commented, following an old adage, that people are at their best in the Christmas season.

From human beginnings on earth, our recognition of the sacred is acknowledged in song. The ancient Hebrews sang chants to the Lord. David puts texts to music and gives the world a beloved heritage of psalms. He speaks forever of the yearnings and laments of the human spirit. His instruments and lyrics of voice allow Hebrew faith a universal currency—a tribal deity has become the God of the world.

After they had sung a hymn, the Evangelist recalls, Jesus and his guests at the Passover meal went down the southern precipice of Jerusalem and across the Kedron Valley to an Olive grove known as Gethsemane.

In the earliest church, the congregation took a direct part in music—doxologies, kyries, allelujahs, and amens. The message of religion has always needed the concomitant of music.

In the sixth and seventh centuries, a great reformation occurs in the church. It is a mixed blessing. The chanting of priests was substituted for the singing congregation, and that was a loss. But the Gregorian chant became the glorious heritage of a church now trying to reach the whole world with a redeeming message—a great gain.

Medieval Germany retained some small participation for the people in the liturgy. In the Easter service, the congregation joined in the kyrie and the allelujah. One such twelfth-century sequence went: Christ is risen, we shall be happy, *Kyrioleis*. Bach used this medieval liturgy in his compositions along with others.

Carl Orff in the *Carmina Burana* uses secular twelfth-century songs that were popular among the people. The common people in medieval Europe engaged in spiritual and humanistic chant whether or not that was sanctioned by the church. Luther, Bach, Mozart, even contemporary composers like Ralph Vaughan Williams draw on this popular heritage in their music for the church. Luther and Bach, for instance, took old German household cradle songs—with their gentle sound and rocking rhythm and wrote hymns and themes within the cantatas. "Puer Natus," the liturgical lullaby, and Luther's "Away in the Manger" are examples of folk customs become the prayer of the church.

Bach believes in this concurrence of word and sacrament, music and message. Prayer and hymn becomes a beautiful synchrony in his hand. Let us consider in this sermon first:

1. Bach's musical artistry,

2. his use of theological sources, and

3. the lasting meaning of his vision.

We have mentioned the influence of the sacred songs of the Middle Ages. The motet shaped by French and Italian instrumental music becomes the cantata. The chorale is formed in the Reformation tradition, principally under the influence of Osiander and Calvin. The basic structures of the preludes are present in the great Lübeck composer-organist Dietrich Buxtehude. The cantata and the passion largely develop out of Italian opera and the Mass, the work of Gabrieli and Monteverdi transmitted to Bach through the work of Schütz.

It may be necessary to explain the reference to Calvin and how he contributes to the chorale. It was the Calvinists, particularly in France, Switzerland, Scotland, and Hungary who insisted that the people and not just the clergy sing in the church. Immediate transparency to the presence of God without an intermediary was demanded.

Sometimes the baby was thrown out with the bath by the Calvinistic insistence to be rid of all mediating and instrumental trappings. In this sense, Fidel Castro was a good Calvinist when he insisted that Christmas be banished on the communist island. Scotland did it for 200 years after the Reformation. This conviction is traced by Charles Garside in his book *Zwingli and the Arts*. The iconoclasm of Calvin and Zwngli, even Luther did not so much deprecate icons, statues and organs as it did to constrain the long-passive communicant to offer praise and faith him or herself.

The theological strains in the work of Bach are also interesting to distinguish. There were four predominant spiritual currents in his time. Current devotees of these movements still claim Sebastian as their own. The medieval Catholic, orthodox Lutheran, pietistic, and mystic movements were vital in Bach's time.

He indeed was a child of the great release of the human spirit that occurred between the Renaissance and Enlightenment we call the Baroque. In the sixteenth century, the doors of the churches flew open to German poetry and song. With aesthetic sensitivity that even Nietzsche had to acknowledge, Luther undertook to reclaim this old poetry and song for the new church. Luther actually saw his work not as *renevatio* but as recovering the ancient and *Volk* church of the Germanic people.

Just as Henry VIII and English Catholic Christians expressed their theology in liturgy and prayerbook (here Cramner's use of Luther is decisive), Luther refashioned the medieval hymns, psalms, and chants into the German tongue as he had the Bible.

In 1524 Martin and Katherina Luther had two eminent musicians as house guests. Conrad Rupff and Johann Walter lived with him as *Kantori Im Haus*. Luther was attuned to matters of art and music, as well as matters of theological import.

Luther's hymnbook, *The Ehrfurt Enchiridion*, became the basis of the German renaissance of church music, as well as the musical and theological basis of Bach's art.

"Music," writes Albert Schweitzer, "is an act of worship with Bach. His artistic activity and personality are both based on his piety. If he is to be understood from any standpoint at all, it is from this. For him, art was religious, and so had no concern with the world or with worldly success. It was an end in itself. Bach includes religion in the definition of art in general. All great art, even secular, is in itself religious in his eyes; for him the tones do not perish, but ascend to God like praise too deep for utterance."[2]

Most of Bach's textual material comes from Luther's fashioning of the biblical faith and medieval Catholic Christianity into the German idiom. The Luther Bible is the basis of the modern German language. When we hear Bach's works, *Christ ist Erstanden*, *Christ Lag in Todesbanden*, we know why the most used books in Bach's library were *Luther's Collected Works*.

---

2. Schweitzer, *J. S. Bach*, 1:167.

## Bach I

As Germany collapses into barbarism and ruin during the sixteenth century, religion alone allows the soul and the "common soul" to survive.

Poetry takes refuge in this bosom of the culture. Nikolai and Franck, seventeenth-century mystics, write poems which Bach later uses. The best known lyric is Caesar Franck's *Jesu Meine Freude*. Franck's *Schmucke Dich*—"Bedeck thyself o dear soul"—becomes the foundation of the splendid Chorale Fantasia that sent Schumann into ecstasy when he heard Mendelssohn play it on the organ.

We also know the Nikolai/Bach hymns—"Now Let Every Tongue Adore Thee" and "O Morning Star how Fair How Bright."

The essence of the mystical theology is that the soul is raptured into communion with God through ecstatic union and participation in the suffering, death, and risen life of Jesus the Savior.

In the great *John Passion*, for example, you feel the pleading pathos as voices and instruments yearn to be incorporated into the life and death of the Jewish Messiah—the *Christos*.

"In the last resort," says Schweitzer, "Bach's real religion was not Lutheran Orthodoxy but Mysticism. In his innermost essence he belongs to the history of German mysticism. The robust man who seems to be in the thick of life with his family and his work and his mouth seems to express something like comfortable joy in life, was inwardly dead of the world. His whole thought was transfigured by a wonderful, serene longing for death"[3]

The pietist movement is strong during Bach's lifetime. Here the emphasis was on gentle inner pastoral life. Paul Gerhardt is the principle pietistic writer utilized by Bach. Among his poems "O Sacred Head Now Wounded" and "All My Heart this Night Rejoices" are beloved pieces in their Bach transcription.

To summarize—Bach builds his spiritual vision on preexistent musical material and theological sources. He took secular songs, street songs, love songs, mountain songs, and lifted them all into sacred beauty.

Bach lived out Luther's convictions and celebrative lifestyle. One night in the Bierstube, Marty opined, when asked about his retrieval of ribald pieces—"Why should the devil have all the good tunes?" Today the Beatles stand squarely in the traditions of Luther and Bach.

In theology, Bach brings the strains of medieval simplicity, Renaissance vitality, post-Reformation mysticism, and Lutheran pietism and scholasticism into his conceptual faith world.

3. Ibid., 1:168.

## Second Sermons

What shall we say in conclusion of the significance of J. S. Bach?

Although we may concur that the deepest significance of Bach is transfiguration of death into life, one of his lasting meanings is to show the high worthship (worship) of the gift that we have been given to offer the world. Bach superinscribed all his compositions with the words *ad majorem dei gloriam*.

Our secular gifts—those things we do well, the crafts, drawings, the skills, the professions, the duties of maintenance, care and service—all have a high dignity, a divine dignity.

We have succumbed in our time to utilitarian, bottom line ways of valuing our lives and activities. College students talk of marketable skills. The ancient university charter, established at its beginning in the church, knowledge and goodness, has reverted to functional values in trade centers.

Bach dealt with the tensions between production and beauty throughout his life. As a young man—already acknowledged to be a musical genius—he was auditioned for the music director's job at Jacobi Church, Hamburg (where our family once worshiped). He didn't get the job. Records later show that the man who received the position made a contribution of 4000 marks to the church.

Bach records in his notes that the winter of 1728 was most trying for his large family. The weather had been mild, and there were very few deaths, yielding very few honoraria. Work was so slow, he writes, that all he was able to accomplish was writing the *St. Matthew Passion*.

Paul Hindemith in his bicentennial lecture on Bach's birthday speaks of the high spiritual excellence which appears in lowly human form: "The research of recent decades has in many respects showed how in Bach's case towering artistic eminence and personal indistinctness, superhuman intuition and pettiness are mingled. The mythical being is beginning slowly to change back into a human being, the glittering hero is growing into a lovable fellow citizen notwithstanding all his failings, the statue of stone and bronze is becoming flesh and blood."[4]

In very human form, Bach practiced what can only be called a sublime vocation. He could have pursued dramatic oratoria à la Handel that would have been more profitable. He rather followed the more humble churchly route, which extolled the commonplace. Yet he was a pioneering explorer. Hindemith writes of this venturous aspect of his life and work:

---

4. Hindemith, "Johann Sebastian Bach 400." Lecture given on September 12, 1950 at Bach Commemoration of the City of Hamburg.

# Bach I

"Bach was one of those heroes of far-reaching and long-planned strategy whose accomplishments men may recall long after if at all: those who, in full awareness of the consequences, undergo deadly scientific experiments for the benefit of mankind; explorers with the certainty of personal failure; inventors who know that their own discoveries will kill them or bring them neither thanks nor acknowledgement. Had not Bach been of this kind, our world today would be the poorer by one of the most astounding intellectual achievements of man."[5]

Hindemith continues:

> To understand him we must try to put ourselves in his place. What can a man do who technically and spiritually has climbed to the highest rung of artistic production attainable by mankind? . . . He has arrived at the end, he stands, as the old Persian poem says, before the curtain that nobody will ever draw aside. For this ultimate attainment he must pay a dear price: melancholy, the grief at having been bereft of all former imperfections and with them the possibility of proceeding further.
>
> This way out of despair and suicide is barred for him who has climbed to the summit. Only one move is open to him: to apply the means he is wont to use in serenely enhancing, serenely adorning his steepest, narrowest, humblest abode on the outermost plateau. With this his creative work turns into sublime creativity, his craftsman's proficiency into philosophical vision.[6, 7]

---

5. Ibid.

6. Ibid.

7. Comments: Second Pres. was a great incubator and encourager for a preacher who loved good music in the classical tradition. For most of my professional life, I have begun the day with the best in sacred music—e.g., "With Heart and Voice" (WFMT), Kings College Cambridge Evensong of the cathedrals of France and Germany. That Second Pres. graced the city with one of the finest organists—Michael Shawgo and an opera quality quartet—insuring an inspiring theological and liturgical service every Sunday has made an indelible mark on my life. Every book I have written is full of references to music.

# 4

# Bach II[1]

THE AMBULANCE CARRIED AN eighteen-year-old black boy into our emergency room. He had pulled a knife on an old man as he carried home his groceries on Chicago's Westside. Unexpectedly, the old man pulled out a gun and shot him in the head. He died the next afternoon at the University hospital. That same day on the northwest side, a seventy-six-year-old man buried a pocketknife in the arm of a nineteen-year-old girl as she at knifepoint sought to relieve him of his watch and money. Two old men now join Bernie Goetz, the New York subway vigilante, as our newfound heroes. In the words of a rather bizarre film, *Network*, they were "mad as hell; they refused to take it anymore."

We wonder how we will respond to the ravages of human malevolence, to inevitable sickness and suffering, to uncontrollable natural evil. Do we resist, resign ourselves, or take some intermediate posture? If we follow Niebuhr's prayer, how do we know what things can be changed, cannot be changed, and where do we find appropriate courage, serenity, and discerning wisdom to know the difference?

---

1. The following meditation was first offered seven years earlier than our preachment at Grace Lutheran Church in River Forest during the performance of Bach's Cantata 93:
    *Wer Nur Den Lieben Gott Lässt Walten.*
    Homily at Grace Lutheran Church, Sunday Feb. 17, 1985.
Text: 1 Peter 3:8–18.

# Bach II

These questions pressed in on the mature, forty-six-year-old Johann Sebastian Bach, as in 1731 he composed the cantata *Wer nur den lieben Gott lässt walten*. Bach wanted to express both the daily trauma of our existence and the underlying trustworthiness of God.

To express this distress and hope he was persuaded by Picander to use both modern free verse and the traditional chorale cantata form. Before him he had two texts prescribed for the fifth Sunday after Trinity. A rather astute theologian, Bach knew the mysterious synergy and momentous power that was often found in the juxtaposition of lectionary texts. In the Gospel for the day, Jesus says to Peter "launch out into the deep water and let down your nets!" Peter answers, "Master, we have toiled all night and come up with nothing. But at your word we will fathom the depths again." The night was followed by morning. The empty hold was filled. The yield was abundant.

The second text was more difficult. Set against the background of the violent persecution in Asia Minor in the first century, the Epistle from First Peter says in sum:

As you suffer for the right, you are drawn into the depths of Christ's passion. In that anguish, you will participate in the joy that was set before him, enabling Him and you to endure the cross. Live therefore in mercy, sympathy and gentle submission, a patient example to your persecutors. Don't live in aggressive retaliation to the wrongs of life, yield to Christ who did not resist evil, but overcame evil in His good cross.

Two passages: both baptismal texts in the life of the early church. Peter, the frustrated fisherman, letting down his nets into the depths of Galilee's sea; Peter the Apostle, about to be let down to his death in inverted crucifixion, planted deep in Rome's soil under Nero. The toil of life, the torture of death, and all the tragedy in between, Bach lifts it all, the baptismal drama of life and death, into the illuminating and fortifying presence of *Christus Victor*: the one who suffers on in victory for the regeneration of this, his world.

Bach also had before him the Luther Bible texts of Psalm 55, one of those whining songs of complaint about the persistence of woe ". . . They rise against me . . . lie in wait for me . . . talk the city like dogs to jump and devour me . . . Lord consume them in your wrath . . . have the last laugh . . . You are my strength . . . my defense."

In these Psalms as in the book of Job, evils are personified as enemies who conspire against us and attack us. All the evils of life are enemies with faces . . . violent thugs . . . rapacious merchants . . . belligerent nations . . . negligent landlords . . . faithless friends . . . misunderstanding family members . . . bad genes . . . cruel circumstances . . . degrading poverty . . . icy blasts . . . malignant diseases . . . meaningless deaths . . . We cry out to the Lord, our avenger: Expose them Lord; bring them down. "I won't take vengeance into my own hands, I promise . . . but only if you're sure that you will heap burning coals upon their heads." "Damn you, you'll pay for this" . . . so natural, so satisfying.

Remember how the embattled Job exulted, "I know that my avenger liveth and He shall stand at last upon the earth." Handel understandably preferred the mistranslation "redeemer." Can you imagine a soprano rendering the gentle aria, "I know that my avenger liveth"? Anyway, I'm afraid the avenging Lord is not the avenger we crave.

He's not Mr. T, the A-Team, Dirty Harry, or Rambo. He doesn't attack our enemies. He doesn't even show them up. He doesn't obliterate the pain of life. His Word is very much out of step with the modern theodicy. You know, "Why did God do this to me? Why do bad things happen to good people?" All these arrogant theodicies are based on gods Kierkegaard called "ludicrous twaddle." Our little systems have their day.

We insist on identifying cause, imputing blame and demanding recompense. His Word . . . be still . . . wait his leisure . . . suffer God to guide you.

Psalm 55 concludes, "Cast your burdens on the Lord. He will suffer for you." Of course, fight back when it is seemly . . . but do your own part faithfully. As Mahalia Jackson says, "Don't ask God to bring the mountain to you when your feet and legs are in good shape." Above all, trust in him all your ways.

Victory over evil is moral response, not passive resignation nor violent retaliation. In Gandhi's word, it is *satyagraha*—love force.

In the cantata after this first statement of Neumark's classic hymn by the choir, we have the recitative, one of the most powerful passages in the Bach repertoire. Here Bach asks where release and rest is to be found. When neither fresh dawn nor gentle evening can satisfy our tears, our only joy is *christlicher Gelassenheit*, letting go to the leading on of Christ.

A number of us in this congregation, indeed the congregation itself, is active in "Project Ten: Health Medicine and the Faith traditions." We recently had a letter from a North Dakota physician who belongs to the Hutterite faith community. This small religious group has their own philosophy, indeed practice, of medicine. This doctor explained why his community could not accept modern Western medicine. Why? *Gelassenheit*, he said, you refuse to let go. You fight, you attack disease and death . . . you refuse to give up, to give over, *Gelassenheit*.

You know giving up is one of the loveliest Christic words in our vocabulary. In crucifixion, Christ gave up his life. Giving up has become an ugly, chicken word to us. Yet Bach poses it as a magnificent and strong virtue. *Er trägt sein Kreutz mit christlicher Gelassenheit*.

In this passage that primitive chorale is joined to free-flowing verse to express the grip of inescapable circumstances the plaintive wandering of abandon, all undergirded by the ultimate constancy and security of God.

In Albert Schweitzer's words, we have *cantus firmus* and *insouciance*, literally, carefreeness. Then follows the tenor aria and the women's duet and the theological contrast of two moments, two hours. The hour of trial—*kreuzes tunde*, the hour of joy—*Freudestunde*. God's grace does not abandon us in our hour of need.

He knows us intimately: our every thought, every need. He knows what is happening to us; He does not allow affliction to overwhelm us, he sends his help. *Er kennt die rechten Freudestunden*. At exactly the right moment—the *kairos* moment, his appointed time—he leads us through. As Paul wrote to the church at Corinth, "God is faithful to his promises. Like Job he will not allow us to be tested beyond our power to remain firm. He will give us strength to endure and will offer a way out" (1 Cor 10:13).

That God allows suffering may be offensive to the theology of some. It certainly is offensive to those who worship the indulgent god Jane Russell called the "cosmic sugar daddy." But if God is really the one Jesus showed us, then all reality, history, politics and natural day-to-day life process is cruciform in its inner direction. This means that time and space are the environment for creation's straining and suffering toward redemption. God himself intimately participates in the vicissitudes of life.

Nothing befalls us, said my teacher, Helmut Thielicke, that has not been allowed to pass the eyes of Christ and come on through to us. All that happens to us is therefore purposive.

I think we can go beyond this and say that God is in the midst of our life, stirring up crisis. He is redeeming each of our lives day by day. He is renewing his creation and that involves disruption and pain. Scripture, from the Psalms and prophets to Peter, teach us that God is a refining fire, a shaker, an overturner. Falling into the hands of the living God is trouble, not rest. Crisis in the biblical sense means opportunity; God is breaking down our securities in order to break through, to bring new creation and genuine comfort.

The deepest meaning of our texts and the cantata is that God, through Christ, is doing something in this world. His dealing with us as persons, churches, and nations, drawing us into turbulence and tumult. This, of course, is the meaning of baptism.

All the great crises we face today ought to be seen in this light: God disturbing the comfortable orders of our life; racial tensions, poverty, drought and famine, international relations, ecological collapse, nuclear holocaust. In all challenges, God is testing us to see how we will respond to his righteous will—his way of justice in the world.

This is the theology of Lincoln's Second Inaugural Address (note the resonance of this passage with the Scripture texts and the cantata):

> If we shall suppose that American slavery is one of those offenses, which in the providence of God must needs come but which, having continued through his appointed time, He now wills to remove, and that He gives to both North and South this terrible war, as the woe due to those by whom the offenses came shall we discern therein any departure to those divine attributes which the believers in a Living God ascribe to him? Fondly do we hope . . . fervently do we pray. . . yet if God wills that it continue until the wealth piled up by the bond-mans two hundred and fifty years of unrequited toil be sunk, and until every drop of blood drawn with the lash shall be paid with another drawn with the sword, as was said three thousand years ago, so still it must be said: The judgments of the Lord are true and righteous all together.[2]

Words of vengeance, violence, some say, but down deep were words of gentle resignation, *Gelassenheit*, magnanimity and peace. In this spirit in the tenor recitative Bach takes violent geophysical images to show the stillness deep inside. He creates a tempest around Peter, the rock. Like the night the storm came up on Galilee, master rescue us, lest we perish . . . peace be still . . . Peter is always at the eye of the storm.

The song trembles with thunder, storm clouds and heat, wind and rain, even the convulsion of death . . . at the silent center of the whirlpool is stillness, calm, serenity. The peace of Christ. If the winds and waves are

---

2. Quoted in Sandburg, *Abraham Lincoln*, 772–73.

under his sway, if the heights of the heavens and the depths of the seas and all that pass through obey his will . . . if even the sparrow's fall is comprehended, the fishes' catch is surely Christ mediated and then turbulence is nothing less than his call, suffering his appointed hour, and sickness, his glorification.

Elijah discovered at Mt. Horeb, God is not the wind, not the fire, but underneath, throughout, within. He is the still small voice.

Six years after Bach's death, another composer was born, one who restored the vision of a caring God after the assault on belief wrought by the Lisbon earthquake of 1755 in the same way that Bach had restored belief devastated by the Black Death of the late Middle Ages. Mozart heard the truth of Bach's message and knew the same inner secret of life. That is why he and his contemporary Mendelssohn sponsored the revival of Bach and Handel, those two geniuses born in 1685, that *annus mirabilis* whose tercentenary we celebrate this year.

Karl Barth called Mozart and Bach two of the Church's great theologians. Why? Because beyond immediate and ultimate evil, which Whitehead called cosmic discordance, they heard a divine harmony. "Mozart," writes Barth, "had heard and causes those who have ears to hear, even today, what we shall not see until the end of time; the whole context of providence. As though in the light of this end he heard the whole harmony of creation to which the shadow also belongs, but in which the shadow is not darkness, deficiency is not defeat, sadness cannot become despair, trouble cannot degenerate into tragedy and infinite melancholy is not ultimately forced to claim ultimate sway. Thus the cheerfulness of this harmony is not without its limits but the light shines all the more brightly because it breaks forth from the shadows."[3]

"Break forth o beauteous heavenly light and usher in the morning . . ." Both Bach and Mozart allow the shaft of divine light to penetrate this shadowy world. Although Hindemith argues that Bach was never able to penetrate through the veil because of confinement to the musical forms of his age—yet he lifted those earth-forms to such perfection that he achieved his own stated life purpose "to create harmonious euphony to the glory of God and for the instruction of his neighbors."

When he heard Mozart's serenade for thirteen wind instruments, Salieri cried, "I was frightened—it was the voice of God." "God needed Mozart to get himself into this world."

---

3. Barth, *Church Dogmatics*, III/3, 297-98.

And so with Bach—allow him now in this cantata to get God into your world. Bach's final word is about God getting into our world with story and salvation, melody and harmony: "*Sing, bet und geh auf Gottes Wege.*"[4]

---

4. Comments: The theologian/music appreciator/preacher has also had his hopelessly idealist nature burnished by clinical and street experience. The bioethical world has helped me grow into a more realistic and "down to earth" witness to the faith. Persons like Martin E. Marty and the Lutheran hospitals of Chicago were also part of this good influence.

# 5

# Mozart[1]

MOZART IS INDEED A genius for all ages. One of the most beautiful pieces of music of the ages is the Vatican Vespers—*Miserere Mei*—a sixteenth-century chant composed by Allegri that is known and loved around the world. The tradition goes that the piece was confined to being performed only in the Vatican—nowhere else—upon pain of excommunication. Mozart visited the Vatican—heard the piece and was so moved that he memorized it —had it performed back in Middle Europe—and the lark escaped its cage.

One of the season's leading plays—in London, New York, or Chicago—is Peter Shaffer's *Amadeus*. Add this drama to the message we may draw from our scriptures and we can draw instruction for our own faith and life.

In *Amadeus*, which would become an award-winning film, Shaffer contrasts the life stories of two composers of the eighteenth century: Antonio Salieri and Wolfgang Amadeus Mozart.

In his notes Shaffer says he was prompted to write the play by an entry from Beethoven's diary claiming that Salieri, a modestly endowed composer, who gained Kappelmeister status over Mozart for himself, actually

---

1. Sermon preached at Second Presbyterian Church, Chicago, June 14, 1992. Texts: Jer 31:1-3, Joel 2, Luke 12, John 1:1-5. Also preached with exerpts from Mozart's Adagio in E flat from the Serenade for 13 Wind Instruments, K 361 in St. Peters Parish Anglican Church in Wolvercote (Oxford), England [assisted in sound by our son—Keith].

29

poisoned the young Amadeus. Building on this conjecture, Shaffer builds his narratives of the two lives.

Salieri, whose obscure pieces are often played on local classical music stations, was a plodding, pedantic, average composer—who was famous.

Mozart is the creative, inspired genius for his, and perhaps all, centuries, yet he dies destitute, despairing—and lay finally in an unmarked grave.

Let us explore the lives of these two music men today and think about our own lives. The contrast is deliberate and helpful. In the short run, and to everyone's eyes, the one is popular and successful—the other vulnerable and a failure. But the foolishness of God is wiser than the wisdom of men.

Almost every person whose life has had a lasting impact for justice and good in the world was at one time a failure: Mozart, Lincoln, Michelangelo, Jesus, Job, Moses.

Salieri is a righteous and religious man; Mozart—a rascal. Salieri remembers the night when he dedicated his life to God and music:

> I wanted to blaze like a comet—already when I was 10 a spray of sounded notes would make me dizzy almost to falling! By 12 I was humming arias and anthems to the Lord. My one desire was to join all the composers who had celebrated His Glory through the long Italian past . . . Every Sunday I saw Him in the Church, painted on the flaking walls. I don't mean Christ. The Christ's of Lombardy are simpering sillies with lambkins on their sleeves. No, I mean an old candle-smoked God in a gambling robe, staring at the world with dealers eyes. Tradesmen had put him there. Those eyes made bargains, real and irreversible; You give me so, I'll give you so! No more, No less!. . . I went to see Him the night I left Italy forever. I made a bargain with Him myself. I was a sober 16, filled with a desperate sense of right. I knelt before the God of bargains and I prayed through the smoldering plaster with all my soul:
> 
> "Signore—let me be a composer! Grant me sufficient fame to enjoy it. In return I will live with virtue. I will strive to better the lot of my fellows. And I will honor you with much music all the days of my life!" As I said Amen, I saw his eyes flare—
> 
> "Bene—go forth Antonio—serve me and mankind and you will be blessed"
> 
> "Grazie"—I called back—"I am your servant for life"

As Blaise Pascal has noted, we have all made our wager with God and the calculations of the universe—tit for tat—goodness for grace—deeds for deserts. The only problem is that when we demand our image of fulfillment—success and fame—when we insist on our own story and negate the divine story, we end up with something hollow and grotesque. At the end of his life in the film *Amadeus*, we find Salieri a deranged, pitiful old man—trying to slash his throat.

On the other hand, Leopold Mozart pushed his prodigy son into the limelight. His father dedicated him Amadeus at birth—God's Love. He is paraded to perform around Europe—writes a concerto at four—a symphony and opera at fourteen.

Then the trajectories of the two careers transect in Vienna. In bitter envy, Salieri suppresses the career of the young Mozart, only casting more glory on Wolf's work as he offers the tedium of his own.

In a moving passage from Shaffer's play, Salieri listens for the first time to Mozart's music—the Adagio from the Seranade in E flat for 13 wind instruments.

Salieri speaks (shaking to audience):

> ...and then, right away, the concert began I heard it through the door—some serenade: at first only vaguely—too horrified to attend. But presently the sound insisted—a solemn Adagio in E flat ... it started simply enough: just a pulse in the lowest registers—bassoons and basset horns—like a rusty squeezebox. It would have been comic except for the slowness, which gave it a sort of serenity. And then suddenly, high above it, sounded a single note on the oboe. It hung there unwavering—piercing me through till breath could hold it no longer, and a clarinet withdrew it out of me, and sweetened it into a phrase of such delight it had me trembling.
>
> The light flickered in the room. My eyes clouded! The squeezebox groaned, and over it the higher instruments wailed and warbled, throwing lines of sound around me— long lines of pain around and through me—ah, the pain! Pain as I had never known it. I called up to my sharp old God "what is this? ... what"! But the squeezebox went on and on, and the pain cut deeper into my shaking head until suddenly I was running—dashing through the side-door, stumbling downstairs into the street, into the cold night, gasping for life. What, what is this pain? What is this need in the sound? Forever unfulfillable yet fulfilling him who hears it, utterly. Is it your need? Can it be Yours?
>
> Dimly the music souned from the salon above. Dimly the stars sone on the empty state. I was suddenly frightened. It seemed to me I had heard a voice of God—and that it was issued from a creature whose own voice I had also heard—and it was the voice of an obscene child!

## Second Sermons

Salieri once spoke of Mozart's *Magic Flute* in contrast with the tedium of his own operas. "I take the gods and make them commonplace—he takes the commonplace and makes them gods."

The contrast between Mozart and Salieri helps us sharpen our own goals and identity. Are we open to the creative and new, or are we stuck in the old and weary?

Salieri finally comes to curse his calling and assault his indulgent deity.

> Capisco! I know my fate. Now for the first time I feel my emptiness as Adam felt his nakedness. Tonight at an inn somewhere in this city stands a giggling child who can put on paper, without actually setting down his billiard cue, casual notes which turn my most considered ones into lifeless scratches. Grazie, Signori! You gave me the desire to serve you—which most men do not have—then saw to it that the service was shameful in the ears of the server. Grazie! You gave me the desire to praise you—which most do not feel—then made me mute. Grazie tante! You put into me the perception of the Incomporable—which most men never know!—then insured that I would know myself forever mediocre... Why? What is my fault? ... him you have chosen to be your sole conduct! And my only reward—my sublime privilege—is to be the sole man alive in this time who shall clearly recognize your incarnation! Grazie, e grazie ancora.[2]

"God needed Mozart," cried Salieri, "to get himself into the world." That is what God wishes from us—entrée into the world.[3]

The story of Israel is the grand story of God "letting himself into the world." Joel prophesies in a day when Israel had its doubts. Cyrus the Persian King had allowed a tattered remnant of the people to return to Jerusalem from Babylon—now Iraq. Zerubabel had constructed a flimsy temple where Solomon's architechtural gem once stood. The old glory was gone—the majestic kings, the inspired prophets. Surely God had abandoned them—this after choosing them—*Grazie Signori!* Now locusts were infesting everything in sight. The Greeks and Romans would soon sweep away those short-lived kingdoms—the first ever dedicated to the Lord Jehovah. Soon they would lay in ruins—like present day Gaza.

But Joel glimpses another destiny—another story.

"The days are coming when I will pour out my Spirit."

"All flesh will know that I am with you."

---

2. Shaffer, *Amadeus*, 1–38.
3. Ibid., 10.

## Mozart

"You will know that I am God—and none other—you will not be put to shame."

Salieri shamed Mozart all his bitter life—perhaps shaming him to an early death. Yet even in his sickness and dying, he crafted works of beauty and divine power: *Don Giovanni*, the seranades, *Magic Flute*, the immortal *Requiem*. While Salieri's works are time-bound, Mozart's will live for all eternity.

In Luke, Jesus describes a farmer who lives filling his silos with grain—finding there his eternal contentment. Then comes that fateful night—"this night your soul is required of you—what now for your silos?" What you do—do well, says Jesus, and give away what you have.

Grabbing on and hanging on to what you have—acquisitiveness—is really death-boundedness. It is necrophilia—fatal attraction to things—to non-life and anti-life. Ironically death itself is ultimate letting go and release. Here we relinquish all we are and all that we have achieved and acquired to the greater reality of God. Penultimately we are invited in grace to die into the life service of others. We discover and find ourselves as we expend ourselves for others.

Luke presents an interesting twist to this Jesus word. Matthew presents it as a negative command: "Do not lay up for yourselves treasures on earth where moth and rust corrupt and thieves break in and steal" (Matt 6:19–20). Be rich toward God, not stuff, pleads the physician. Carry a sturdy purse—one that is well worn with frequent openings.

Christians belong to the order of the well-worn purse. Ours is a sustaining narrative of generosity and gratitude. Gratitude is acceptance of who we are—unique, unprecedented, and never-to be repeated gifts to the world. Freed from self-absorption and fascination we are freed to look beyond and above.

"Do you see yonder wicket-gate?" asks evangelist in Bunyan's *Pilgrim's Progress*.

The man said "no."

Then said the other,

"Do you see yonder shining light?"

He said, "I think I do."

"Then keep that light in your eyes and go directly thereto."

"So shalt thou see the gate."[4]

Karl Barth summarizes our convictions about Mozart:

---

4. Paraphrase from Bunyan, *Pilgrim's Progress*.

I must again revert to Wolfgang Amadeus Mozart. Why is it that this man is so incomparable? Why is it that for the receptive, he has produced in almost every bar he has conceived and composed a type of music for which "beautiful" is not a fitting epithet: music which for the true Christian is not mere entertainment, enjoyment or edification but food and drink; music full of comfort and counsel for his needs; music which is never a slave to its technique nor sentimental but always moving, free and liberating because wise, strong and sovereign? Why is it possible to hold that Mozart has a place in theology, especially in the doctrine of creation and also in eschatology, although he was not a father of the church, does not seem to have been a particularly active Christian and was a roman catholic apparently leading what might appear to us a rather frivilpus existence when not occupied in his work? . . . Mozart shows us that creation praises its master.[5]

---

5. Barth, *Church Dogmatics*, 297–98. Comments: Karl Barth's habits of highly disciplined biblical and theological work, highly political parish work—and beginning each day with the bible in one hand and the newspaper in the other—while a disc of Mozart wafted through the air and joyously filled the house—has been a pattern I have believed in though imperfectly mimicked for fifty-plus years of ministry. Though not a musician myself, I have been surrounded by my wife, Sara, and our family, which always supplied my pretense.

# 6

# Gandhi[1]

"...Who saves his life will lose it, Who loses his life for my sake and the Gospel's will find it" —Matthew 10:39 and parallels

THE WORD IS SATYAGRAHA—LOVE force or life force. The origin is that linguistic source of all speech (action)—Indoeuropean (Sanskrit) and ayravedic. It was embodied in Jesus and the early Christians, the medieval Jews against awesome Byzantine oppression, Amerindians against the ferocious Puritans, Gandhi against the British Empire, M. L. King Jr. and the freedom riders against the Klan, the Palestinians with their slingshots against the Americo-Israeli Empire. Sometimes—as with the Indian Raj—it worked; other times it backfired and led to outrage and slaughter.

Gandhi lay near death. This, his latest death fast, again held India's 350 millions, indeed the whole world, in frightened suspense. Previous fasts had led to justice for the "untouchables" and had won independence from England. Now India itself was threatening to break apart along religious lines: Hindustan, Islamistan, Pakistan. Mahatma—the great soul, lay weak and shriveled. The streets flowed with the blood of violence and killing. Gandhi would die in fast in order to bring peace. Again and again, the leaders of India tried to dissuade him, saying things were getting better. But

1. First preached in The Riverside Presbyterian Church, Feb. 27, 1983.

his instincts and finely honed spiritual intuitions knew that there was still revenge in the air.

Finally, they gathered around his pallet and convinced him that peace had come over the land. There was Nehru, Jinnah, and Ali Khan. The leaders all promised reconciliation.

The fast was broken. Gandhi himself orchestrated the thanksgiving service. A passage was read from Bagavad Gita and Quran. Then this unlikely circle of Hindu and Muslim leaders sang the hymn "When I Survey the Wondrous Cross." The filmmakers found this event so incredible that they omitted it. For a brief instant (perhaps ninety minutes, as with the truce in Gaza in 2014), the three major world faiths, Hinduism, Christianity, and Islam, may have glimpsed God, his Rama or Kingdom, and in that momentary vision found their cohumanity.

Abul Kalam Azad, a Muslim congressman, brought a glass of orange juice, and the saintly scholar rose up to resume those final, fateful days of his work.

Of all people, Christians should know about satyagraha, the love force of active resistance to evil. We should know about the paradoxical secret of the cosmos, that suffering and death taken into oneself bring healing and life to the world.

Satyagraha is found in the mystic strain of many primitive religions and Old-Oriental faiths. It is embedded deep in the ancient Indo-Eurasian tradition from which Hinduism springs. It is found in Jesus and Paul, Thoreau, Ruskin, and Tolstoy. In recent years, it has been embodied unto death by Gandhi in 1948 and Martin Luther King in 1968.

Gandhi's book *Satyagraha* is the classic treatise on the subject. Satyagraha is a way of life that involves a style, a power and a love. It is an intimation of the Eternal—the leitmotif of our set of sermons.

The qualities of love, non-revenge, non-retaliation, and forgiveness positively oppose our inclinations toward avarice, aggrandizement, and aggression. If we are to achieve sanity in our mad, mad world, we must swiftly recover that ancient wisdom which Erik Erikson called "Gandhi's Truth." It is a soul force, a spiritual power against which all the physical power and force in the world cannot stand.

We live today in a world threatening to break apart at the seams. Materialistic greed threatens to cast the world to the brink of social chaos. As Mike Royko famously declared even here in Chicago, the city's motto *Urbs in Horto* (city in a garden) has become *Ubi est Mea* (where's mine). Only Gandhi's truth about frugality, fabricating, and fasting can save us.

We are threatened today by our obsessions with power. These obsessions, rooted in paranoiac fear, conspire to do us in in one of two ways; either through the cataclysmic extinction of nuclear holocaust or more probably the simmering emaciation of economic deprivation caused by misallocation and maldistribution of wealth—"not with a bang but a whimper." Only Gandhi's truth of gentle nonviolence in the soul and society can save us.

Then finally, we are threatened by alienation and violence among and between people. Gandhi's truth alone enables us to identify with and suffer with one another.

Consider three dimensions of Gandhi's Truth.

Look at the world around us. Gandhi's truth redefines wealth and poverty. The inequality and disparities of wealth today are unconscionable. The distance between those who live in greed and those who suffer in need is stark and always rising. Some of us stand in long lines in New York City ironically to get a $100 ticket to Dickens' *Nicholas Nickleby* followed by a $200 dinner while others lie on the streets, huddling on the grates hoping that escaping steam will warm them into the cold night. They shiver through the night homeless, hopeless, helpless. In Chicago, twenty thousand line up, some all night, seeking two hundred ten-week jobs while we middle-class surburbanites recite our myths of welfare laxity—you know "they buy steaks with their food stamps while we eat hamburger."

Meanwhile, our President Reagan, in his off-stage moments, reminiscent of Nero, sits back at his comfortable California ranch, reading his newspaper, and is more focused on want ads than human want.

Actually Mr. Reagan has a heart. We all do. We are all touched by human suffering in certain moments. But we all too readily fall back into the more customary apathy and neglect. We need to constantly realize that private benevolence needs to be matched by public provision. The soup kitchens and warming centers in Youngstown, Detroit, Pittsburgh, and Chicago are well and good. But the answer to crisis is not merely charity and momentary largesse from those who have much. We need long-term solutions which go to the root causes of the problems. What is needed is Christic and Gandheic transformation of the social order. Christian faith without structural transformation and justice is neither Christian nor faith.

John Calvin stated it long ago—two hundred years before Karl Marx:

"God wills that there be equality among us. No one should have too much and no one too little."[2]

Yet we frantically pursue prosperity, success, and gratification. "What shall it profit a man," spoke Jesus in words that Gandhi loved, "if a man gain the whole world and lose his soul." Three themes in Gandhi's life style commend themselves to us:

## FRUGALITY

Frugality is the great virtue of the Puritan. It means simple non-consuming, non-avaricious life. In that mountain sermon which so profoundly changed our notions of peace and power, literally transforming the lives of Tolstoy and Gandhi, Jesus said, "the pure in heart shall see God." The puritan faith, that spiritual and moral tradition we might profitably reconsider in our own time, believed in frugality leading to sharing. For Gandhi, that simple life had to do with diet, meditation, exercise, and habitat. He left this world only with a Bible, two pairs of sandals, and his spectacles. Remember the words of that same mountain sermon, "Lay not up for yourselves treasures on earth, where moth and rust corrupt and thieves break in and steal—rather lay up for yourselves treasures in heaven—where your treasure is there your heart will be also." All of the cookbooks, exercise books, and other self-help manuals that are our stock-in-trade today can be summarized in the simple message: Live frugally and be well. Simplicity begets philanthropy. This was Gandhi's first lifestyle lesson.

## HANDIWORK

One day he took his London worsteds, cast them into the dustbin, and wrapped himself in a handmade dhoti or loincloth. This made Winston Churchill exclaim: "Who is this half-naked fakir coming up the steps of his majesty's viceregal palace?" It was then that Gandhi began his lifelong litany on the *charka*, the spinning wheel. In full view of Britain's massive import of cloths and India's own textile mills, the little man sat at his spinning wheel. It was identified with the earth, with the poor, and with the Fabricator, the *Schopfer*, the Maker of the universe.

---

2. Calvin, *Commentary on 2 Corinthians*, 679.

Today we must find ways to sustain personal creativity and cottage industry. We must never surrender to the gods of technology and industry. If you have a chance, visit the inner-city kids at Providence-St. Mel High School in Chicago. Listen to the yearning and courage in the souls. Hear of their ardor for the community. They do not sit stupefied in front of video games screens.

To be true to Gandhi we cannot become Luddites—machine crashers. He might have been very caught up in the ingenuity and facility of the computer. It can be a great force for information and for the construal of the data of reality, enhancing and intensifying our God-given intelligence. Gandhi's point on the spinning wheel is that hard work rising from intellectual virtuosity binds us to that great busybody, mother earth, to the redemptive toil of others and to the great Force who is "Making all things new."

## FASTING

Fasting is also a response to materialistic temptation. Fasting is not only cleansing and healthful, it is an act of responsibility to the creator God who leisurely works making all things "good." It is a protest against starvation in the abundant world. It is also the vehicle of *Visio Dei*, which is self awareness.

On March 23, 1940, Gandhi awoke in the night in terror. The trembling then led to serenity. He records:

"About 12 o clock in the night something wakes me up suddenly, and some voice—within or without, I cannot say whispers—'Thou must go on fast'—'How many days,' I ask. The voice says again '21 days.' When does it begin,' I ask. It says 'you begin tomorrow.' That kind of experience has never happened before or after that date. If ever there was a spiritual fast, it was this . . . It is not possible to see God face to face unless you crucify the flesh."[3]

His teacher, Jesus, put it this way—"This demon is only cast out by prayer and fasting."

Gandhi was the Schumacher—the "small is beautiful" urbanologist of his day. He was the forerunner of the Chinese commune, the Israeli kibbutz, the colonial American village. The essential concept: smaller units, ownership and participation by those who do the work—better living conditions.

---

3. In Jones, *Mahatma Gandhi*, 85.

E. Stanley Jones, the great Christian missionary and close friend of Gandhi, summarizes:

"Mahatma Gandhi with his spinning wheel is a protest and a pull. The Mahatma sitting athwart the road to rapid and ruthless industrialization says to the greedy-for-profit-hordes: Thou shalt not create millionaires and misery palaces along with mass production, yielding mass poverty."[4]

Today we are witnessing the ugly effects of an accelerating centrifugal-centripital laissez faire economy. The rich are fast growing richer and the poor are almost done in. The middle class is rapidly disappearing while an enormous polarity of very rich and very poor classes has become a moral disgrace. The top 1% of the world's population owns more wealth than the bottom 40%. The discrepancy and divergence is especially marked in Gandhi's countries—India, Pakistan, and Bangladesh and in Africa, South America, and the impoverished sectors of the Middle East and Asia.

On the global scale, the poor, sick and hungry are dying—en masse—and their exsanguination, like Abel's, cries out to God. Here in America, most are losing their holdings and a small circle is joining house to house and field to field—as reprehensible as Israel's splintering, concentration, usurpation, and occupation of Palestine. Stokely Carmichael's dictum again is born out: "When the imperial colonialist came we had the land and they had the Bible. When they left we had the Bible and they had the land. It is the old 'Golden Rule'—Those who have the gold make the rules."

Still, protectionism and isolationism seems to be our craving. Last year (1981) I was in New York City when dignitaries were celebrating the ninety-fifth anniversary of the Statue of Liberty. Someone was reading the words of Emma Lazarus:

"Give me your tired, your poor, your huddled masses yearning to breathe free. The wretched refuse of your teeming shore..."

At that very moment, the Atlantic tempest indeed tossed up onto the Florida shore the bloated, blue bodies of the shipwrecked Haitians.

> Send me your homeless, tempest-tossed to me
>
> I lift my lamp beside the golden door

Gandhi's vision can save us from the illness and sadness that comes from concentrating and hoarding earth's abundance. It can lead us to the

---

4. Ibid., 25.

grace of reciprocal sharing and delight. "I have come," said Jesus, "to give life, life in abundance. This is my body and blood given for you drink ye all of it."

Gandhi also redefines power for our age. The ultimate force in creation is the force of peace and liberation. The Hebrews called it *Shalom*, Jesus called it the "kingdom of God." Gandhi called it *Rama*. Detractors derided the early Christians as "those who have turned the world upside down." Part of our continuing moral task is to challenge those governments that use power to oppress and dehumanize people. Whether it be Haiti or El Salvador, Germany, Russia, or America, we should lend our soul force to what Lowell calls the power behind the scaffold—where wrong "seems to hold sway"—and that power which sways the future. On Christmas Eve of 1941, Gandhi wrote to Hitler pleading that the Führer cease violence and make peace, but unlike Montbatten and the British, in Germany there was no conscience to which nonviolence could appeal.

Today East and West are arming to the teeth. The Soviet Union and the United States have also turned the rest of the world into military economies. Israel and Syria, England and Argentina confront each other as protégées of the super powers. Even Gandhi's lands of India and Pakistan have threatened (and now become) nuclear powers—as has Israel.

But there is good reason for hope. As I revise this thirty-five-year-old sermon, Israel and Hamas/Palestine have declared a cease-fire after a one month war that has turned Gaza into rubble and ruins. Today —August 5, 2014—Palestinians and Israelis cautiously rise from their shelters and find flower markets on the streets.

Catholic bishops now seem to pause in their nationalistic postures and exert soul force in the service of peace. Chicago's Cardinal Joe Bernadin exerted a coherent and convincing witness. Even in the fervent and evangelical Presbyterian church, peacemaking now becomes the imperative. Even exclusivistic, Christian empires like Russia and the U.S. recover the deeper impulses of Roger Williams and Jefferson and Tolstoy and Marx with the irenic justice these traditions carry. Perhaps this residue of peace can uncover in politics, with Gandhi, the undergirding peace of God.

Yet we continue to cry peace, peace, when there is no peace. The truce of God is a strenuous and rigorous phenomenon. It is only enduring when it abides in the divine peace.

Gandhi was in jail when his son, Manilel led the march on the salt works at Dharasana. Wave after wave of committed, nonviolent demonstrators fell under the police clubs. They did not raise a hand, did not protect their heads. It was soon evident that the battle was over. Five hundred were permanently injured; two had died. Those who were beaten had won the war. Webb Miller, of the *New York Times* wrote the report that stunned the world:

> In complete silence the Gandhi men drew up and halted a hundred yards from the stockade. A picked column advanced from the crowd, waded the ditches, and approached the barbed wire-stockade . . . Suddenly at a word of command scores of native policemen rushed upon the advancing marchers and rained blows on their heads with their steel-shod lathis. Not one of the marchers even raised an arm to fend off the blows. They went down like ten pins. From where I stood I heard the sickening whack of the clubs on unprotected skulls. The waiting crowd of marchers groaned and sucked in their breath in sympathetic pain at every blow. Those struck down fell sprawling, unconscious or writhing with fractured skulls or broken shoulders . . . The survivors, without breaking ranks, silently and doggedly marched on until struck down.
>
> They marched steadily with heads up, without the encouragement of music or cheering or any possibility that they might escape serious injury or death. The police rushed out and methodically and mechanically beat down the second column. There was no fight, no struggle; the marchers simply walked forward till struck down . . .[5]

Mahatma wrote:

> We will match our capacity to suffer with their capacity to inflict suffering. We will match our soul force with their physical force.

> We will not hate, but neither will we obey.

Social action without piety (moral strength) is as dangerous as piety without social action. "Faith," said the Apostle James, "without works is dead."

Finally, the test of moral and spiritual authenticity is our relationship with the neighbor. Gandhi's truth redefines *community*. Gandhi went out to live with the outcasts. He rode third class on the train. His life was deeply shaped by the old Gujarati hymn:

---

5. Quoted in Fischer, *Life of Mahatma Gandhi*, 273.

> For a bowl of water give a goodly meal;
> For a kindly greeting bow thou down with zeal;
> For a simple penny pay thou back with gold;
> If thy life be rescued, life do not withhold;
> Thus the words and actions of the wise regard;
> Every little service tenfold they reward,
> But the truly noble know all men as one,
> And return with gladness good for evil done.[6]

"Return no man evil for evil," said the Apostle Paul, "As much as it depends upon you live at peace with all" (Rom 12:12, 18). The spiritual secret of all high religion is simple: If love can only break out in some small corner it will soon overwhelm the whole world.

In September 1910, shortly before his death, Tolstoy wrote his disciple Gandhi these words:

> The longer I live, and especially now when I vividly feel the nearness of death, I want to tell others what I feel so particularly clearly and what to my mind is of great importance, namely, that which is called "passive resistance," but which in reality is nothing else than the teaching of love uncorrupted by false interpretations. That love, which is the striving of human souls and the activity derived from it, is the highest and only law of human life; and in the depth of his soul every human being, as we most clearly see in children, feels and knows this; he knows this until he is entangled by the false teachings of the world.

This was proclaimed by all—by the Indian as well as by the Chinese, Hebrew, Greek and Roman sages of the world. I think this law was most clearly expressed by Christ, who plainly said: "In love is all the law and the prophets."[7]

The desperado stood over the Mahatma, His dark eyes bristled with vengeance and shame. "He was just this tall," the poor Indian sobbed. "They killed my son and I killed their little girl. What must I do?" Gandhi looked up from his mat. Though weakened by his fast his eyes shone full of mercy. "Take yourself a son," he said softly, "one who has lost his father, 'about so tall,' and raise him a Muslim."[8]

6. Ibid.
7. Tendulkar, *Mahatma*, 122–23.
8. Ibid.

Comments: Theology and preaching needs to be biographical. A real story of a real person seems to best grab and motivate people. Toyohiko Kagawa, Francis of Assissi, Teresa of Avila or Calcutta, Dietrich Bonhoeffer, M. L. King, Abe Lincoln, Daw Aung San Suu Kyi in Burma rivet our attention to what is good, just, and holy. All rivet our attention to One who is good, just, and holy. That One who stands or sits among us, even the eternal Christ.

# 7

# Calvin[1]

## CALVIN ON GOD

CALVIN HAS REASONED AS carefully and forcefully as anyone between Aquinas and Barth that the reality of God is apperceived in the realm of nature through reverent human consciousness (*Betrachten*: Johannes Kepler). Humans are *Homo Religiosis* —beings who bear the divine Image in the world. By our very nature therefore we are receptors of the mediating knowledge (Logos) of God within the scientific substance and historical cognizance of what we call the cosmos—the created world. Memory and hope, awareness of within and beyond, flesh and mind, body and spirit are the media within which this inner constitutive reality of reality becomes actual in the world. Hereby God, as the rain, ever sheds "fresh drops" of God's very substance and action into the earth.[2]

---

1. [To better orient this series of sermons, reference must be made to the father of the Presbyterian faith, John Calvin. Calvin takes the Bible, church fathers, Augustine and Aquinas and weaves in his oeuvre, especially the Institutes of the Christian Religion (1533), the belief system which will become significant national churches in France, Hungary, Scotland, Bohemia, England (Puritanism and Wesleyanism), The US (Puritanism), Germany ( Reformed), Switzerland (French sector), South Korea, and other places in the world—e.g., the Baptist world.]

2. Cicero, *Tusculan Disputations*, 20–30.

## CALVIN ON "THE UNITY AND SOVEREIGNTY OF GOD"

i use the adjectives "Unity" and "Sovereignty" (following Calvin) to deal with the "Name" and "Nature" of God in a manner faithful to the Abrahamic faiths ("simplicity" was also used early). These stipulates are embedded in the primal creeds of Judaism and Islam and remain fully intact in the Triune God of the Christian movement. As a Christian, I believe that the God and Father of the Lord Jesus Christ, Yaweh and Allah, is the One God who reigns in unity—sovereign over creation. All access from humans to God and from God to humans proceeds through this One Logos channel who is the life and breath of humanity and all creation. My students will be aware that my Logos epistemology (Christology) of this corridor of contact is wide, mysterious, and variegated—wherever Son, Messiah, Spirit, or Wisdom is manifest.

Throughout this essay, I will use these rubrics (Unity and Sovereignty) as summarial catchwords for the wider meanings of the Being, Action, and Nature of God. God's being is truth. God's action is good. God's nature is lovely. These "Transcendentals" (Good, Truth, and Beauty) can be compared to Aquinas' fundamental ideals, which he derived from Aristotle. These correspond with the truth, good and beauty of Aristotle and the most primal Eurasian and worldwide philosophers—the "One and the Many" of Hinduism, Buddhism, Taoism, and indigenous world faiths. I begin to believe, as I approach my seventies, when one can be forgiven for being a fool, that Christianity, in the first centuries of its era, wrongly assumed that Judaism denied Logos ("God also"), and Judaism wrongly assumed that Christians denied the One God and were not monotheists. And Christians wrongly assumed that Jews did not know the rich unity and multiplicity of God. Islam may be appearing in God's providential history to ameliorate these frightful mistakes.

## CALVIN AND THE INTERFAITH PRESUPPOSITION

Thomas Aquinas presents what is perhaps the fullest exposition in history of the truth of God. Aristotle, Avicenna, and Augustine are his equals. Calvin, Wesley, and Barth come close. Thomas knew the truth knowledge of Scripture along with that found in these first three thinkers. For him, there were two dimensions of divine truth—revelation and reason. Truth resided both in things and intellect (*rebus et intellectus*). God comprehends all truth as its creator and consummator and invites humans to the delight of apprehension. Jesus as human and divine (as Yaweh) is the Way, Truth, and Life (John 4:16).

As I write in the summer of 2014, a Medill-trained (Northwestern University) journalist is beheaded in ISIS-invaded Iraq or Syria. Al-Qaeda blames American bombing on the border of Kurdistan where hundreds of bodies are dismembered. Sunni kill Azeri, Israelis kill Muslims in Gaza, and retaliation follows retaliation. Interfaith justice and peace is the imperative of God, not exceptionalism and revenging murder. Calvin, in some contrast to Luther, brings such interfaith respect into human history.[3]

---

3. Comments: Calvin and his lawyer-contemporary Ignatius in Paris established the great orders of preachers which persist to this day. Calvin is heard in every Puritan field preacher or Wesleyan circuit rider, Ignatius in every Jesuit evangelist in Uraguay and the present Pope. My own substance and style as a preacher is shaped by Calvin as he offered his homilies to the French congregation in Strasbourg, formed the women's and children's choirs, and instructed the lawyers under his post in Geneva.

# 8

# Sonday[1]

TODAY IS NEW YEARS in the church—first Advent—the beginning of Christmastide.

As snows again whirl over the landscape and as the seasonal malaise called "blue Christmas" settles in, even today as Christmas carols waft through the Riverside Mall, where the great car-obelisk shimmers in the wind or along State Street in the Yuletide which began on Halloween, the vague anxiety comes again and the lection texts of the day don't help unless we take a closer look.

On that Son-Day when the "cloud man" or the "man of the sea" as he used to be called—when the Son of Man comes—scary things happen.

Your own family betrays you—children their parents and parents their children, children devour their own flesh and blood. Maybe this is what Fukuyama means by "the end of history." In the bitter world we have created, this is what we seem to have done to Muslims in Iraq, for example. The familicidal and fratricidal impulse of apocalyptic end-times is witnessed in the Middle East today, where in Palestine Hamas attacks

---

1. Sermon preached on the Son of Man, First Advent, 2005, Riverside Presbyterian Church. Texts : Mark 13: "When the Son of Man comes . . ." Ezek 1: "and above the dome above there was something like a throne, in appearance like Sapphire, and seated above the throne there was someone like a "human being"(*Bar Enash*), Aramaic, translated "Son of Man").[Here read Scriptures Ezek 1, Mard 12, Luke 21.] The following sermon, also later preached at Second Pres., struggles with Calvin's vision of God and human affairs. For this entire sermon use Wink, *The Human Being*.

Fatah, in Iraq the U.S. superintends a genocidal cleansing of Sunni by Shia, in Afghanistan the Taliban vie with tribals, and in myriad locales in Africa all hell breaks loose with Muslim north against Christian south, all against the grim backdrop of HIV and excruciating poverty. All this is the terrible cost of apocalyptic unrighteousness, where human lives are easily sacrificed for oil, cashmere, or diamonds, or shall we say the great God—Cash—and that's not HEEEEre's Johnny.

In Mark's little apocalypse (ch. 13), the skies grow dark—earthquakes, famines clouds—and by the way kids—that man's not Santa! Its not "here's Johnny" not Jack Nicholson or any other son of saint Nick—it's not Mr. Potato Head or Dora the Explorer in the Macy's Day Parade blowing along 34th street—its the Son of Man—the Human One—so terrifyingly terrific.

The nations rage—wars and rumors of wars.

Herod's great Jerusalem temple will fall as the stones tumble down.

The fig tree withers and the veil of the temple is rent in twain.

When all this happens look up and see the "sky man"—the "Son of Man" descending in the clouds.

The setting for whatever was said in Mark 13 and Luke 21 was Jesus looking on the temple with some disciples, probably from the west side as the sun set on the glorious edifice—and here's the first rub—did Jesus foresee the destruction of the temple thirty years before it actually happened? All I can say is Augustine's—"I don't know." As they look on, Luke reports Jesus' comment on the widow's mite—the poor woman who gave everything she had—this indeed may be the meaning of the text—a comment on the land-grabbing and life-taking Moloch machinery of empires who think they have the right because they have the power. Jesus, it seems, is looking upon the glory of the city of Jerusalem—glory that will be blacked out with the Romans imperial army crushing of the insurgent nationalist and religious rebels—and he weeps, knowing a peace that the city could have had if they only had faith. "Get out now," he cried, "as fast as you can, flee to the mountains, and pray it does not come in winter."

You may have heard in this particular season the musical setting of this scene by Billings and William Schumann in the *New England Tryptich*:

"When Jesus wept the falling tear in mercy flowed beyond all bound

When Jesus groaned the trembling fear seized all the guilty world around."

In this tumultuous and cataclysmic crisis on earth which is then, always, and now, we are chided in our faithless distress and counseled to wait in expectancy and trust. Like the widow with her mite, we are to do the faith, live the righteousness, pray for the kingdom come.

Don't prepare your defense in advance.

Don't worry what you will say when the tribunal summons.

You will be given the words of witness in that hour.

And here again—that text:

"The hairs of your head are numbered, not one of them will be lost."

So what shall we make of this disruption of our complacent holiday?

We can find here, I believe the seasonal miracle of true faith and good life we hear in Aaron Copland's *The Tender Land*, written for the 1953 commission by Rogers and Hammerstein:

> The promise of living is born in thanksgiving
> The promise of caring is born in the sharing
> Our love with our neighbor

On first hearing, this son of man thing may sound like Dick Butkus coming to coach the Montour, PA high school football team, kicking butt to get the team back on the road to glory. It's like the Texas bumper sticker: "Jesus is coming again and boy is he mad" (or words to that effect). But look closer. Of course, the good news of the season is found in the high Christology:

> Joy to the world, The Lord is come. Let earth receive her King.
> Come let us adore him, Christ the Lord.

You may wonder about the sermon title. Sonday is a play on words something like the lead song in that musical *Hair* that gave the sixties one of the first religious rock hits: "Let the Son Shine In."

On this Sunday, look at the biblical setting, theological meaning, and ethical imperative.

## I.

Son of Man is a mistranslation. Words like Ben Adam in Hebrew and Bar Nasr in the Aramaic Jesus spoke are better translated the "human one" or the "human being." The phrase is used 100 times in the Old Testament (not nearly the 6000 times the name Yahweh is used), 90 of those occur in Ezekiel, and 50 times in the New Testament, almost all in the Gospels. It is the only title that Jesus uses for himself. Others of his followers, Paul and the early church, call him *kyrios*—Lord, Son of God, Christ or Messiah, King or God. If the son of man phrase points to the humanity of God, "Son of God" points to the divinity of man. In this compound, Jesus as Christ is fully God and fully human.

The call to worship today is from Psalm 80, and our Old Testament reading echoes the signature text of Daniel 7, "I saw in the night vision one coming like a Son of Man in the clouds of heaven." This echoes the great vision of Ezekiel 1, which may lie behind Genesis 1 and much more of the scripture: "

"Above the dome was a throne looking like sapphire and seated on the throne was one who looked like a human being—a son of man."

To Mark's passage, just read, add Luke 21. Here the tribulation and trauma—the fall of the temple, the pretenders to be messiah, the great calamities on earth and in heaven, then the armies surround Jerusalem, then when you see the son of man coming on a cloud with power and glory Lift up your heads—your redemption is coming near.

Matthew adds two important texts:

The disciples are sent out to the towns of Judea. The apostolate of the Gospel begins . . . The persecutions set in. These are the messianic tribulations and the travail of disciples in the world. "When they come after you, move on—before you've gone through all the towns of Israel, the son of man will come." The trigger of the coming seems to be the confrontation of proclamation and opposition.

Then in ch. 25, the great final judgment scene "when the son of man comes in his glory, he will gather the nations before him and he will sort out the sheep from the goats—I was hungry and you fed me, naked and you clothed me," and so on. In his award winning book—*The Human Being*—Walter Wink summarizes the biblical teaching on the son of man:

"The most audacious claim of Christianity—more audacious than the resurrection or that Jesus was messiah was that . . . the human being had entered Godhead as a human being. God wanted to become human so that humans might become like God. Instead of an angry, punishing, tyrant God now has a human face, one who comes near us, full of mercy and understanding being one of us."[2]

In Wink's theology, God's fundamental nature and purpose, given this vision of Ezekiel, is to make us fully human and deliver us from oppression and domination.

2. Wink, *Human Being*, 166.

This advent deliverance comes from patriarchy and the oppression of women and children; economic exploitation and the impoverishment of entire classes of people; hierarchical power arrangements that disadvantage the weak while benefiting the strong; the subversion of law by the defenders of privilege; racial superiority and ethnocentrism. All this is the secular concomitant to salvation and deliverance from sin and death. In Christ, we are saved from sin to righteousness—from death to eternal life.

Jesus, the human one, in other words, delivers us from the powers of the world.

I agree with this liberation theology. My own theology of the "Beloved Son" is shaped by the suffering and rising lamb of God as understood in the Akedah, the Abrahamic reading of the Jewish, Christian, and Islamic sacrificial and sacramental heritage. This parable conveys the mystery—the sacrament—of the death and resurrection of the "Beloved Son." Here Jesus, the fully human One, fulfills all righteousness in his love and life offering—yet without sin. This theology is found in the signature hymn of Advent, Charles Wesley's "Lo He Comes on Clouds Descending" which has, in its original Moravian setting, this verse:

> Lo, he cometh, countless trumpets, blow before his bloody sign
> Midst ten thousand saints and angels, see the crucified shine
> Alelujah, welcome, welcome, bleeding lamb.

However conceived, in Jesus' first and final coming as portrayed in the lections for this day something ominous and portentous is going on in heaven and on earth. Some heavenly crisis is being felt here on earth. Some earthly miracle is storming the gates of heaven.

## II.

This biblical overview leads us on to the theological meanings of the son of man. The church has always taught three things about God and God's coming to us. This threefold faith suffuses all Christian Scriptures, creeds, hymns, and popular piety. We worship one who was and is and is to be. In the letter of Hebrews, Jesus Christ is the same yesterday, today, and forever. If you prefer action to being, Jesus is the one who came, who now reigns, and who will come again. Creation, incarnation and eschatology, the teaching of future and final things, is the doctrine at stake.

# Sonday

In this season we sing "O Come, O Come Emmanuel"—God with us. We can't climb up and reach God. We once tried that at Babel and the world has come crashing down on us ever since. We can't force God down. We can't confine or define God. The god of our making is always a false god. God in Christ must come out across eternity to us. God must enter our world as he did in the Christ Child—the daughter of wisdom, the son of man.

That sad yet satisfied Christ—Georges Roualt's Jesus—that face so human—still abides on that sapphire throne.

Karl Barth sums up this theological meaning. "The church's recollection is also its expectation. Its message to the world is also the world's hope. Jesus Christ, whom the church knows, but not yet the world, comes to meet the church and the world. He is the measure by which the whole of creation and every person is measured."[3]

And Barth again: "Jesus Christ's having come, would answer to what we term the past. But how inappropriate it would be to say of that event that it was past. What Jesus suffered and died is certainly not past; it is rather the old that is past, the world of man, the world of disobedience and disorder, the world of misery, sin and death. Sin has been cancelled, death has been vanquished. Sin and death did exist in the whole of world history. All that is past in Christ; we can only think back on all that. But Jesus Christ sits beside the father—he who has suffered and risen from the dead. That is the present."[4]

When Barth was dying, his friend Thurneysen came to him. "Are you well, old man?" he asked. "Sicher," of course, he answered. "Er sitz in regiment"—he sits on God's right hand and reigns over all.[5] Bonhoeffer had the same serenity when led to Hitler's gallows; "How are you so peaceful?" asked his guard. "I am baptized" smiled the young pastor.[6]

Now a final word of what this means for us today.

Knowing this secret, we are an Easter people, a Eucharist people.

Christ's suffering and death is his victory and reign. We live therefore in the old color of Advent—the color purple of penance and victory. We

---

3. Barth, *Dogmatics in Outline*, 127.

4. Ibid., 124–28.

5. Personal recollection of Bonhoeffer scholar Burt Nelson, as told to him by Bonhoeffer's sister Sabine Liebholz-Bonhoeffer.

6. Ibid.

also live in the Sarum color of Advent—light blue—the color of the night sky.

For one came among us as like a son of man. He was Miguel de Cervantes's impossible dreamer—one scorned and covered with scars who fought the unbeatable foe, bore the unbearable sorrow—went where the brave dare not go—and the world, and heaven, is better for this.

Amen![7]

---

7. Comments: My preaching is inescapably apocalyptic. This may be its power or its mistake. Hebrew, Christian, and Muslim scripture all seem to be saturated with the apocalyptic, as do the world events sweeping us along in this turmoiled world of ISIS, ebola, immigration, and global warming. The reader will find this theme and tenor in my every word. Does it open or obfuscate? The way of God?

# 9

# Wesley[1]

I REMEMBER THE DISCUSSION well. It was the early 1970s when we were forming the Hastings Center in New York City and the Kennedy Institute of Bioethics in Washington, DC. About the same time I was founding what would become the Houston Institute of Religion's Medical programs and what would become the Park Ridge Center in Chicago. Each of these centers, including your great center here in Indianapolis, sought to explicate and activate the cultural beliefs and values which could guide the surging enterprise of biomedicine and health care. Faith traditions were a part of this cultural cache of values.

David Smith of your Poynter Center wrote the Anglican volume in a series Martin Marty and I edited. At Hastings that day, two Methodist laypersons, Bob Morrison, the head of the Cornell University medical center and Paul Ramsey of Princeton, led the discussion. What set of inspirations, they asked, could have guided early-nineteenth-century England in her science and industry, labor rights, and the abolition of slavery, personal and public health. Could it have been the vision of John Wesley? Yes—the Hastings Fellows agreed—and those strange people called Methodists.

---

1. This meditation is about the impulses released into human life by the spirit of the movement of Wesleyan theology and ethics as it pertains to the realm of science and medicine. It was first presented at the Centennial of the Methodist Medical Center in Indianapolis (1990) and was later used in various sermons. My preaching at Second Pres., Chicago often drew upon these thoughts.

As we met at Hastings forty years ago, it was an exuberant yet foreboding time, much like today: the space program, intractable war in Viet Nam, kidney and heart transplants, genetic and birth decisions, abortion, life-extension technologies, Karen Quinlan, when-to-die decisions, and the agonies of medical triage. Then to all this was added the challenges of providing care from this cornucopia of blessing for the sick and poor, both here and around the world. John Wesley, where are you now when we need you?

In that ambiguous Camelot/City of Lot moment of the 1970s—so full of glory and darkness—both in knowledge and technology—big global issues in the macrocosm were working their way out in the microcosm of people's bodies. Lasers brought about lethal militaristics and life-saving diagnostics. Communications drew the world together and cruelly accented our alienations. While we tinkled out our little Bach preludes on Schroeder's piano, Pig Pen's perpetual black cloud hung overhead. Principles of freedom and self-determination, justice, and altruism arose within the issues of environment and energy, Viet Nam and Israel, minority, women's, and children's rights. All these were all symbolically being enacted in human bodies and clinical decisions such as eugenics, Baby Doe decisions, and "Living-Will" policies. We even used military acronyms such as MOP+WHOP to label cancer chemotherapies.

The great bioethics institutes, including Hastings, were created to address these quandaries. Without Wesley, claimed Morrison, the modern age of hygiene, child health, industrial safety, and public health would have been inconceivable. Cleanliness *was* next to godliness. And the field and street preaching, the "Be ye perfect ethic," the manuals of health maintanence and ministry in urban hovels, added Ramsey, all fashioned a guiding theological vision to supply the worldly commitments. To this my mentor and predecessor at Garrett added virtues learned in his dad's Methodist parsonage in Mississippi: The inestimable dignity of each human being, the pervasive fall that discolored every human thought and action, and uncompromising commitment to justice and care for the sick and poor.

The lawyers, philosophers, and business people at Hastings were skeptical. Even in those days of lingering Eisenhower religiosity, it was clear to most that economic, legal, and technical considerations outweighed the theological. I was not convinced. Had we not learned from Max Weber, who had visited St. Louis in the early century, that it was religious history, the Puritans, Wesleyans, Calvinists, and their religious ethic that decisively shaped scientific history? That parameter—the spiritual/ethical—much more than politics and philosophy, contoured the practical life and death, birth and health judgments that persons made with their families.

Even our post-religious and post-theological at last was realizing its folly and coming to the end of an age of materialistic and positivistic obsessions about what is really going on in this creation. And I use that word on purpose—for that is the secret of what the world is—*the creation*. For Wesley theology is creation, therefore worldly and the world is graceful and full of Spirit. Spirit defines world and world is the setting of Spirit. This is Origen's *Logos*—which is where Wesley starts. We think of the brilliant work of Carl Michelson which was cut off so early—a worldly theology. This essay is indebted to him and to Albert Outler's book on "the Wesleyan Spirit."[2]

Which leads us to the thesis of this paper. Here at the dawn of your new centennial, let me suggest as we close out one century of care and begin another that the Wesleyan Spirit can make us whole and make the whole people well. It can and should continue to invigorate the world with a graceful, incarnational theology

- yielding an inquisitive and reverential science
- a realistic appraisal of evil and wrong in a resplendent world
- a humanistic therapeutics for health care
- and finally, a sympathetic care and justice for the sick and poor in the local and global health care community.

To begin, a few notes on Wesley, his times, his convictions, especially prevenient and public grace, as his impact provides foundations for today's challenges. Some of Wesley's most widely read writings were on subjects like electricity, energy, and medicine. His primitive remedies: a do it yourself health care manual was found on the fireplace bookshelf in most American homes at the beginning of the nineteenth century. Take, for example, his remedy for the seasonal allergies that get us wired up and worn out in this ragweed season. Forget Claritin and Benadryl—just walk up the mountain and submerge in an icy spring pool and viola! Vasoconstriction, par excellence. Among the myriad scholars who have studied Wesley's medicine are my own students, Phil Ott from Evansville and Wayne Martin, one of the circle of Methodist physician-pastors.

---

2. Outler, *Evangelism and Theology*.

In Wesley's time both the blessing and the bane of the dawning age was being felt. Wesley believed that public health, vitamin C, and better food on the table was the basis of our health and well-being. Hobbes' brutishness and brevity of life—where everyone was at war with everyone—was in full fury. Now suddenly William Blake could dream of a paradise on England's mountains green. We could even build Jerusalem amid those Satanic mills. Perhaps even that holy lamb of God would come back to Birmingham. But would he be welcome. Were things getting better, really better? Or was the world, as Reinhold Niebuhr said, getting better and better and worse at the same time. Would Blake's chariots burn out in infernal chaos or would the blessed green vistas of Dickens' loving concern redeem Scrooge's countinghouse or Tulkinghorn's Bleak House? Would the mercenary and military spirit prevail in our world or might a more Moravian mercy and munificence redeem the time? In our day of Abu Ghraib on the one hand and the Lancaster Amish schoolhouse on the other—the choice is stark and the verdict is still out.

The great challenge to Wesleyan theology today is to retain sacred rigor along with secular relevance. As in all mainline Protestant traditions, the Wesley boat is cracking in the middle. As pietistic evangelicalism and rampant secularism propel themselves in centripetal fury in opposite directions from the Methodist tradition, only learned biblical grounding and efficacious practical ministry will call us back and keep us on course. How Wesley Pavilion at Northwestern, Methodist Hospital in Houston—"the house that Mike DeBakey built"—and this center—how they go may index that faithfulness and that future.

## I.

Incarnational theology anchored in grace is the sustaining wind of the Wesleyan spirit. The heart of such a dynamic biomedical theology is a doctrine of "giftedness" grounded in mercy.

Wesley's conversion, a melding of Aldersgate and the fear and trembling decision to step out into field preaching, was in Outler's words, "a conversion from passion to compassion, from being a harsh zealot of God's judgment to a winsome witness to God's grace, from a censorious critic to an effective pastor."[3] His synergic call to holiness and witness was framed

---

3. Ibid., 104.

by his Lord's Isaianic vocation to preach to the poor, to heal the brokenhearted, and bring deliverance to the captives (Luke 4; Isa 61).

In an important new book, Harvard philosopher Michael Sandel claims in *The Case Against Perfection* that genetic engineering now poses a threat as it assaults human dignity and curtails compassion.[4] We not only scope out and mitigate, but now diagnose and treat genetic disorders—eliminating and correcting imagined flaws and guiding life trajectories toward conceived perfections. But our practice of medicine, he claims, is not undergirded by an adequate philosophy of medicine.

Here we face another challenging aspect of Wesley's biotheology of the human condition and capacity. We need today an adequate realism of human sin as well as an idealism of the human prospect. For such a challenge, Wesley is the man. He helped get us into this perfectionist game, and he has the grace-centered theology to see us through.

When Wesley posited perfectionism from his study of the Sermon on the Mount—"Be ye perfect, as your Father in heaven is perfect" (Matt 5:48)—he was drawing on Origen and the Eastern fathers—anticipating sinless and good beginnings and original immortality—but he also knew Jerome and Augustine—the Latin fathers—who accented our flaws, finitude, and frailty. I think that Wesley swayed from one side to the other as he rode along on his horse—reading. And he got it right. Unlike the modern Methodist reactionaries called the "Circuit Riders" who prompted Halford Luccock to observe "I'd like to see those fat cats on a horse"—Wesley and his riders sensed a subtle blending of these apparently paradoxical truths helping us see, as Hans Jonas showed, that finitude and frailty is blessing, that weakness is proleptic strength.[5] If we could only see through appearance to reality we might see glimmerings of "face to face" in that dark mirror. But here and now we have no abiding city. As Augustine and other great preachers always opined, we remain the pilgrim people of Haran, Horeb, the Herodium and Hajj—always living in tents, ever besieged—Bedouins ever blessed by the desert's night skies and refreshing oases. As Hoagy Carmichael inferred, from his home in the city where we are meeting, Bloomington, Indiana, he was a little bit at home everywhere, yet still searching.

In a secular version of this paradoxical wisdom, Sandel proposes that we see our differences as gifts—what we could call in the Wesley vision elaborations of divine imagination and creativity—works of providential

4. Sandel, *Case Against Perfection*.
5. Jonas, "Burden and Blessing."

and prevenient virtuosity. Steroids can make us all Sammy Sosa or Barry Bonds hulks. Growth hormone or cloning can create lots of Michael Jordans—at least in genotype—but can they really?—or should they? Phenotypic uniqueness in the spirit of grace are mysteries of diversification and spontaneity in what C. S. Lewis, after Wesley, who further wore his bench for him at Christ Church, Oxford—called the divine Tao.[6] This way of health and life—giftedness—what Sandel calls "persistent negotiation with the given," even the acceptance of suffering and mortality—is the clue to our humanity and our divinity.[7]

Wesley glimpsed Hebrew and Puritan perfectionism hopefully—not as manic utopianism and cookie-cutter uniformity but in divine giftedness. My favorite text on this scriptural messianism is in the concluding Jewish Yom Kippur service.

> One late afternoon, Rabbi Joshua ben Levi found Elijah standing at the entrance to a cave.
> "When will the Messiah come?" he asked.
> Elijah responded, "Ask him."
> "Where is he?"
> "At the city gate."
> "How will I recognize him?"
> "He sits among the diseased poor. All of the others loosen every one of their bandages at the same time and bind them all again. But he loosens and binds the bandages over his sores one by one. For he thinks: Perhaps I will be needed: I must be ready to go at once."[8]

The messianic secret, the secret of the hidden mystery of health and disease, life and death is "With his sores we are healed"(Isa 53, Luke 1).

Today the vestiges of Hebraic, Hellenic, and Puritan perfectionism have become an inordinate drive for improvement—blaming and suing, wanting and demanding, failing to reach an ascetic rest—Bach's insouciance—"*Ich habe genug*"—we bring unending vexation to the world. We need to recover the inherent giftedness of the given in our sabbatarian heritage, an Abrahamic faith, not be so manic as we seek to change the world.

In international life today, the enemies of Wesley's Anglo-America are those we call insurgents, "radicalized Muslim," Al Qaeda, the evil empire.

---

6. Lewis, *Mere Christianity*.
7. Sandel, *Case Against Perfection*, 24.
8. *Jewish Prayer Book*, 73–74.

As we welcome the newest and last Harry Potter, we need to remember Gandalf's wisdom in *The Lord of the Rings*: "Other evils there are that may come . . . yet it is not our part to master all the tides of the world, but to do what is in us for the succor of those years wherein we are set" (book 5, ch. 9)—a most Wesleyan sentiment.

Some weeks ago now, an Iraqi doctor, along with several medical colleagues from Saudi Arabia, Jordan, and India, led an aborted bomb attack on London and the Glasgow airport. Britain, which wisely refuses any more to use mythic Manichean words like insurgents, "Muslim extremists," "war on terrorism," and "evil empire," and prefers a more Smylie espionage designation, "international criminals," quickly discovered that this Iraqi doctor had watched his parental home destroyed and his parents killed by the American invasion. As I have tried to show in a set of books on war and medicine, war against disease, against death, against enemies, are dangerous construals, and we need to discover something of the Semitic, stoic, and Islamic grace sanctifying the given. Wesley, though so provincial in many ways, was able to look so deeply into grace that he could "look East" to see Tao, to see into Gautama's vision of the old, the sick, the suffering, and beyond—to an active serenity of grace.

To sum up our first point on the Wesleyan spirit of an incarnational theology of grace, I have argued that an animus has been released into world history which is formed in the half millennium of theological history from Wycliffe to Wesley, a highly creative energy, divine and demonic, thrilling and treacherous. The guiding antidote against the destructive side of the ambivalent energy is Logos/incarnational wisdom embedded in Abrahamic, messianic, Hikmah—a decalogic, akedic Tao that guides our believing and living in the *way* of cross and resurrection, justice and mercy. Wesley saw this in his brilliant vision of salvation and social justice, of faith and works intextricably united in holistic endeavor. Here because of the all-sufficiency of grace, amelioration and acceptance comingle. Teilhard de Chardin captures the equipoise: "We must fight against disease and death with every fiber of our being for that is our divine destiny. But when in the course of events death (or disease) becomes inevitable, we must experience the paroxysm of faith so that death becomes the falling into a greater life."[9]

Messiah, Hikmah, Wisdom, Way, Truth, and Life. Jesus, recall, came with the awesome prophetic annunciation to give sight to the blind, mobility

---

9. Teilhard de Chardin, *On Suffering*, 62.

to the lame, release to the oppressed and laughter to the brokenhearted. A jubilee!

As hoosiers in this great company, you celebrate a century of medical ministry and contemplate the next, you will surely reflect on a checkered history: KKK, Herman Muller, Alfred Kinsey, Baby Doe. There are the great experiments: New Harmony, Mayor Bill Hudnut's Indianapolis; you even have Peyton Manning's Colts—unfazed even by Chicago's Bears. I trust that the Indiana of Dick Lugar and the Bayh family will ultimately join New York, California, Pennsylvania, and Massachusetts in creating your own comprehensive health care system—especially at the social justice level—to overcome the seemingly unending inertia at the federal level. Such progressive states will seek human dignity in defiance of Michael Moore's *Sicko* and find a place where a brilliant frontier of medicine is joined to universal health ministry for the "least of these."

Your ministry in this medical center will be crucial, as here we pursue Wesley's perfection as human responsibility and care. After the 1970s' Baby Doe cases and the broader genetics revolution, Daniel Callahan deplored an outcome when "we will indeed have descended into the pit if we make genetic perfection a condition for the right to exist."[10] The same will hold as I have shown in a series of books for dying well, living well, eugenics, euthanasia, Muller's eutelogenetics, eupolitics, and the rest of utopic manias. The careful and responsible dream is acceptable, indeed obligatory, for any just and good people. Doing good and finding commonweal involves finding giftedness in all sectors of our existence—not only in church but in commerce, industry, education science, the arts, sports (Hello, Barry Bonds and Michael Vick), and international and domestic affairs. In the spirit of Wesley we can translate grace into custom along the highways and byways of life, thereby redeeming and reconciling the world to its creation.

## II.

Beyond a theology of grace grounding the principle of giftedness; beyond the iconic impulse of that idyll of Isaiah 60 where death will no longer seize children or impede living out one's full life, beyond the aniconic impulse which shatters the false idols which seek vitality or death over given life, the Wesleyan spirit also bequeaths to us a reverential, indeed enthusiastic

---

10. Kevles, *In the Name of Eugenics*.

theology of science. My *Abrahamic Theology for Science* and Alan Verhey's *Theology and the Science of Death* are books worthy of your perusal.

There is a desperate need in the world today to renew the Puritan covenant of science and technology for the end of the protection and enrichment of human life. Wesley felt this to be the vocation of our primary world institutions: church, business, health care, and the state.[11] Calvin had emphasized that human life fulfilled on earth was the glory of God. And on the Luther side, Bach's *Goldberg Variations* show that what is excellent and beautiful, worldly wise, is much more to be desired than conventional religion.

If we can only be liberated from our faithless and inhuman manias to the hegemonic and security state (the biblically demonic quest for empire), we could then and must then redirect the marvelous divine providence into care of the sick and poor (the real messianic mandate), Wisdom, Sophia in the service of life.

If we could massively counter crime through caring education and esteem for the distraught poor; disease through careful prevention and accessible therapeutics; war and strife through justice-grounded peace-making and misery through philanthropy, we could reanimate John Milton's quest—so important to Wesley—of paradise drawn onto the earth. Then the stellar Bethlehem gift might be realized and the Magi praise out of Mesopotamia, Africa, and Asia be heard again—peace on earth, goodwill among all people.

In the next century of your history and that of this nation and our world, the genetic basis of most disease will become manifest. The subtle connection between nature and nurture will be seen. Not only will vaccines and biologicals cover most infections, but most malignancies will yield to the combination of predisposition control, infection management, and environment manipulation. Then will become clear the biblical solemnity: "God saw all that He had made and behold it was good—very good."

For now we must counter the blasphemous actuality of our scientific enterprise and its health derivative serving the few exotically and leaving the many in destitution. The plagues of Africa: AIDS, malaria, river blindness, infant and young adult morbidity and mortality all shake the human fist in the face of the creator who yet pleads, "Cain, where is Abel your brother?"

---

11. In this author's view, Wesley's theology and ethics always come down to concrete actions in specific situations.

Michael Moore's indictment in *Sicko* is pretty much on target. What Paul Starr called the sovereign profession has become a negligent industry, and the poor, uninsured, homeless patient is dumped, even by the best of providers Kaiser, Presbyterian, Methodist, on the streets of Skid Row in L.A. in the middle of the night. Thirty years ago, when Starr leveled his indictment that pretty much insured denial of tenure at Harvard, he showed that it was the Presbyterians and Methodists who cast the deciding votes to turn medical care over to the monopolistic fraternity. Now the complex of business and law, insurance, and pharmacy is diehard committed to keep it that way.

The spirit of Wesley always confounds this usurpation of the ministry of health. What sort of retrieval of his ethos can we make today? It is probably as impossible to recover a church-based health and welfare system that prevailed for centuries as it would be to move in this hyper-capitalist land to a national, universal health care system, the model that the entirety of the developed world now enjoys. We need therefore to find a synergy among private and public endeavors, ecclesial, entrepreneurial, and public efforts. We probably have maxed out now at near 20 percent of the GNP into health. Great investments continue to be needed in medical research, public health care, and mental and child health. We obviously cannot continue to spend such a great portion of the health dollar on diabetes and end-of-life care—over 50 percent.

Our best hope lies in that "enlarged knowledge" of which John Milton and the Puritans spoke where self and family care combines with intimate parish provision (Parish meaning every soul in the city and not the diminished meaning of parish after Hurricane Katrina in New Orleans). To this needs to be added intense public altruism and finally a resolute rejection of the "American way of death." All this needs to be based on Wesley's "experimental knowledge" joined to exacting social justice and provision for the weak and poor. Such ascetic wisdom bound into communal and global solidarity alone can save us from the present disgrace of our being known in the world as a self-serving, indulgent, materialistic people.

In a moving interview in the July press, Anne Marie Slaughter, Dean of Princeton's Woodrow Wilson School, calls for our nation to repent our errors of judgment and misdeeds against our own and the world's people. Katrina and Guantanamo must end. Rather than portray ourselves as the champions of MTV, *Baywatch*, promiscuity, and family disorder, we need to return to our bedrock values of rescue and refuge to the world's refugees, champions of the sublime values of liberty and equality rather than privilege and greed. We need to strenuously concur with President Bush, who, when seeing the pictures of Abu Ghraib, did not say, "How did they get those photos?" but, "That's not who we are." We need to hold him and ourselves to that abhorrence, repentance, and resolve and cry with the Pope, no never again! We need, says Slaughter, to honor the distinguished civilization of Hammurabi, of Mohammad and Moses, and Jesus, the Christ. We must cease denigrating other peoples as insurgents and enemies who may be home-defenders and freedom fighters. We live in one God-given world, where each person and each people is unique and indispensable to the whole, not in Huntington's clash of civilizations where Muslims or now Hispanics are enemies to be subdued.

Wesley knew, as did Luther his mentor, that loss of humanity was a symptom of the loss of God. When Joel Osteen preaches in his megachurch on how to smile or T. D. Jakes speaks of success and prosperity, we realize that mega-religiosity has become a source of mega-immorality. Nietzsche forecast that religion amiss would devour itself. We learn that of the 150 of the graduates of Falwell's Liberty University who work in the federal government, 50 percent are under investigation. So just as cleanliness is next to godliness, godliness is the substrate of morality and the reverse. Paucity of human justice and love exposes the vacuity of religion. "By their fruits you shall know them."

III.

Which leads to our third point of the Wesleyan doctrine of wrong and evil and how this illuminates the phenomenon of biomedicine. On this point Wesley displays a unique blend of Hebraic-prophetic, patristic, Lutheran (especially Moravian), and Puritan influence. He was not a schismatic. He believed he saw the original vitality of Jesus' movement and the primitive church. It was a renewal movement in the English church. Were he a citizen of our world, I believe he would be listening for the heartstrings of biblical, prophetic, Abrahamic faith. Wrong was therefore, like grace, a cosmic and universally natural and reasonable human phenomenon. Like Francis, he preached to all creatures and all tribes: Muslims, Jews, indigenous—even the odd Anglican. Birds, squirrels, and of course, the beloved horses—they were all God's family. His rendering of sin and dissonance within the resplendent creation retains this great secular universalistic currency.

## Second Sermons

I mentioned my work in Houston in the 1960s when I was called to develop medical ministries within the Institute of Religion. Many say that the modern movement of bioethics began here with the pastoral and clinical programs that began with chaplains and nurses in the 1940s. One joy of my job was the liaison with COSTS—the Council of Southwestern Theological Schools. From our position at the center of the world's largest comprehensive medical center, with some forty schools, hospitals, and special institutes, we exchanged wisdom and knowledge with Austin, SMU, TCU, and the other great theological universities of what was then the great frontier of North and Meso-American immigration.

On one of my visits to Dallas, my contact, Albert Outler, called me to his office. He was compiling his massive edition of Wesley's works, and he had come across a sermon that he thought would interest me as a scholar of theology and medicine. It was a sermon on the garden of Eden. Our primal forebears were delighting in the bliss of creation before the curse of disease, dissension, and death had intruded themselves into paradise. Our first parents luxuriated in the knowledge of limitless bounty, the manifold provision of everything for all their needs, except for these strange quarantines, "Do not eat."

The woman picked the pear, a fruit much more succulent and seductive than some coarse and wormy bramley, so intoned the grave and erudite Oxford scholar—now a street and field preacher. Then, Outler says, Wesley suddenly stops and dramatically isogetes: "His heart and the vessels around it started to clog up. There you have it—the beginnings of atherosclerosis."

Wesley's definition of evil is a breath of fresh air and liberating animation for culture in general and biomedicine in particular. It provides a kind of Arminian antidote to the darker side of Calvinism and the genetic fall of Augustine. The doctrine of harmatology and theodicy—sin and evil—bears more directly on health and disease, life and death than any other realm of culture. The enterprise of medicine, must declare, either explicitly or implicitly which problems it chooses to confront and which to accept. Take AIDS and diabetes, substance abuse and sexual diseases, for example. Diabetes, a recent epidemic, can be conceived as an inbred and genetic disorder or the result of misfortunate behavior—the diets of the poor and junk foods. The understanding of causation, i.e., the wrong, influences the treatment options, e.g., screening or behavioral modification and often whether patients are esteemed or disparaged as "trolls." Unfortunate designations of good and evil, e.g., homosexuality, have often stifled medical advance and treated people with injustice, even violence.

The current stem-cell debate is marked by a somber gray mood that says that if you are going to terminate embryos by God you are not going to bring some good out of it for others. Not much better, it must be admitted, than this hyper-Augustinian view is the hyper-Pelagian, which holds that we must bring redemptive compensation out of the horror of global abortion by helping Michael Fox and Christopher Reeves.

An honest, realistic, and ethical doctrine of human responsibility is sorely needed today in medicine and health care. The tendency to blame is widespread especially when it is joined to the right to sue. As we noted earlier, one implication of the doctrine of grace and giftedness is realizing that the given is not necessarily tragic. Our life spans—even our morbidities and mortalities— are not only boundaries and contradictions but are salutary even necessary concomitants of life itself. Hans Jonas wrote an essay entitled "The Gift of Mortality." In Calvin and the Puritans, the doctrine of providence has great merit and comfort in its confidence that "each hair of our head is numbered" and "no bird falls from the sky" without God's knowledge and care.

In health care, we need an active, action-inducing theodicy, one which offers the continuing work of prevention and protection but also acquiesces to an embrace of suffering and death in a cruciform wisdom that Abrahamic faith calls the Akedah. Waking one crisp morning at Walden Pond, Thoreau observed that we ought not to think of winter, with its ice and snow, as a problem to be solved.

The doctrine of fall conjoined to the reality of forgiveness yields a fulsome rendering of redemption. Such rich and searching insight will be absolutely necessary to the fathoming of the enigmas of disease in this coming age of biomedicine. The editor of the journal *Science* projects that the two dominant diseases in the world by mid-twenty-first century will be AIDS and Alzheimer's—irascible, complex, ever-mutating, defying human comprehension and control. Disease in the future will be more like this— hiding from immunological surveillance, resisting therapy. We have traded the easy for the complicated, the treatable for the chronic and incurable. In the next several centuries we may isolate and describe the genetic predisposition and environmental stimulus of most disorders. Then what? Will we eliminate the tainted by screening or by designer reconception and remaking of persons? Will we advance into an era of elective demise—when we each decide when, where and how we take leave, or will we revert to the ritual of the migrating peoples—ice floes and sweeping floods will be frightfully omnipresent in the hot-box future of our own making—one of socially engineered eugenics and euthanasia—that future so terrifying to artist, prophet, and poet.

For these reasons, I commend the depth and penetrance of a Wesleyan doctrine of sin, fall, grace, forgiveness, and new life as an appropriate ethical theology for the unfolding drama of biomedicine. Supplying much of the impulse of a modern theology of Spirit[12] and religious life around the globe (especially the Pentecostal and charismatic movements), theology in the Wesleyan spirit avoids the extremes of sin viewed as chronic and inevitable on the one hand and imaginary as in naïve progressivism on the other. A healthy axiological theology acknowledges our injustices, insensitivities, self-aggrandizements, and persistent failure in what we do and fail to do. Believing in the ubiquity and dynamism of human wrong makes repentance, mercy, reparation, and new beginnings possible.

Especially in health and disease, living and dying, AIDS, and liver failure, behavioral weakness and interpersonal failure, we need to always proffer eucharistic grace, forgiveness, and another chance. When the aforementioned Chicago Bears tanked Tank Johnson this summer when he was stopped late one night on an Arizona highway, supposedly under the influence, they failed to think it possible, because of his past misdeeds, that his blood alcohol might be within acceptable limits, which it was. But his career is finished, and beware Barry Bonds, Michael Vick, Tour de France riders, beware the self righteous, white steed riders with sword in throat mowing down the unrighteous. Wesley's doctrine, though contributory to a Puritan ideology of evil, becomes insidious when only the smile remains of the Cheshire cat, and Americans especially chide, "How wrong of you to think that I could be wrong." Goodbye, Tank. Maybe we'll just have to live with another Colts Super Bowl.

## IV.

The next to last element of biomedical wisdom found in the Wesleyan spirit is that of humanistic therapeutics. Teilhard de Chardin calls this a delicate equipoise between life affirmation and death acceptance. In my

---

12. For this line of reasoning, see Eugene Rogers' and Sarah Coakley's writings on homosexuality.

career I have tried to strike this balance as a faithful response to my mentor theologians of the high Middle Ages, Renaissance, and religious Enlightenment: Aquinas, Luther, Calvin, and Wesley. I have always refused the simplicity of "right to life" or "freedom of choice" on abortion. Freedom of choice to abort a female child is wrong, as is demanding the birth of a child with Tay-Sachs disease. I have simultaneously insisted on the right to live for handicapped, retarded, and critically ill children and elders, and the right to "let die" and assisted dying for those who feel it is a rudimentary good "to give your life back to God."[13]

I testified in favor of what would become the Roe v. Wade abortion decision in the early 1960s. With Father Richard McCormick, I supported the right of the parents of the Danville Siamese twins to withhold treatment, a decision I honor after watching the weaker twin die after three years of round-the-clock suctioning at nearby Misericordia Hospital, but one I regret when I see the stronger son after the separation thriving as a young man. He wouldn't be here if they had followed my advice and the wish of his parents. Only the orthodox doctrine of fallibility offers forgiveness. *Pecatta mundi*: the ubiquity and universality of the "sin of the world" and *non posse non pecatta* (Luther): "It is impossible not to sin."

I supported the morphine-induced terminal coma in the hypothetical case of "Debbie's Dying"[14] in opposition to the giants of medical conservatism and was honored when the thousands of letters from practicing physicians decisively favored that position. This landmark case revealed clearly that such decisions—far from being "no brainers" were deep ordeals of heart and mind, profound mysteries of good and evil—always entailing uncertainty, remorse, and forgiveness. My briefs on Karen Quinlan and Nancy Cruzan were on the side of the "let-die" judgement though, unlike the politicians, I shared no jubilation but only "mysterium tremendum"—a sense of awe before the solemnity of life and death.

On other issues that show the humanistic commitment to therapeutics, I support Oregon's attempt at public universal health insurance—even with a medical triage component. I welcome the movement of other states in this direction: New York, California, Massachusetts, among others. I honor the comprehensive health care systems of England, France, Belgium,

---

13. This idea was shared personally with Vaux by Joseph Sittler. One can helpfully refer to his book, *Nature and Grace*, Philadelphia, Fortress Press, 1972.

14. See my essay in the *Journal of the American Medical Association*: Vaux, "Debbie's Dying."

and elsewhere where our children enjoy excellent care without the terrifying fear of "will I be able to pay?" It is hard enough to be sick. The physician-aided dying in Holland, and informally in other, especially Protestant countries, seems worth exploring, and the initial results are promising in terms of not leading to abuse. I have advocated justice and equal rights for homosexual persons as well as openness in the parish life and ministry of the church.

This generic persuasion grows out of my doctoral research in Germany on Nazi eugenics, euthanasia, and racism, where non-abortion and selective killing displaced therapeutic realism with ideology. That realism of Calvin, Wesley, Barth, and Niebuhr recognizes that we can unnaturally and cruelly prolong the dying process just as we can fail to accept nature's own wisdom about living and dying at life's beginning.

I have tried to live out this realistic Wesleyan humanism even in my own family. My theology has always been clinical—personal and pastoral rather than idelogical. At the familial level, I approved of my great aunt's—the nurse-anesthesist Edith's—decision to give morphine to assist the dying of my great-grandparents when they were decrepit and in intense terminal suffering. I concurred with our physician-son and nurse daughter-in-law's decision to bring to birth our first grandson with XYY. He's now a strapping fourteen year old—a promising artist like his uncle, and a mean tennis player. I agree with our daughter and son-in-law in Antwerp to risk a pregnancy even though she carries in recessive stat a serious genetic disease. I supported our other daughter in her marriage—I performed her wedding—even with serious risk of familial diabetes: her little daughter, Aislinn Moira, we babysit with delight as I write this essay. In case you wonder about our grandaughter's name, her dad is Irish, and we all carry at least five lethal genes.[15]

---

15. Comment: Here again my hearers will feel the imprint and impact of the biomedical sphere. This was the world which opened its doors to me when I found the struggle to navigate the church too discouraging. It kept me in range of the places where spirituality, ethics, love, and justice were unfolding. It gave me a calling card, a livable income and a proximity to the hearth-fires of faith now well into my eighth decade.

# 10

# Come Labor On[1]

WHO'D HAVE THOUGHT—CHIEF JUDGE John Roberts—a tried and true conservative—now appears on an Obama "Hope" T-Shirt. The Affordable Care Act—derisively called "Obama Care" by Wisconsin tea-sipper Paul Ryan—now Veep candidate—has been upheld by a 5–4 vote. Roberts has joined the Court moderates against the Scalia-led conservatives. The air waves exult with two strange messages from familiar messengers: "I am Obama who cares" (Obama) and "On day 1 I will repeal Romney care . . ." whoops "Obama care" (Romney). The historic achievement in this, the only advanced nation in the world that does not provide universal health care, is that the story is more about John Roberts than either Obama or Romney. It proves again that no one party has the corner on what Paul Krugman calls cruelty or decency, economic vice or virtue. Most pundits say that Roberts was trying to safeguard the integrity and reputation of the High Court or protect it from the negative reputation she has incurred by recent divisive decisions. Some even went so far to predict that as the court rapidly sank in public respect, that it was closing in on three strikes and you're out. After the contentious Bush v. Gore decision (2000)—a far too political decision for our preeminent body of justice—the court decided

1. September 2, 2012 at Second Presbyterian Church, Chicago and Highland Park Presbyterian Church, Sept 9, 2012.
Texts: Ps 28: 4–9; John 6: 26–32; Jas 1:17–27. Hymns: "Come Labor On," "God is Working His Purpose Out."

that, instead of the people, they would decide who would be president. To this was added the now widely contested judgment—the Citizens United decision (2012)—where big money and super-pacs would now be released to so influence elections that we could confound our most basic liberty—the vote itself. A closer look at this court decision at the end of June showed that Judge Roberts was more likely coming from some other place. He actually believed that health care for all was good, the right thing—required by civilized people.

I believe that he drew on an instilled theological and ethical heritage which he had learned from the ethical excellence of Catholic social teaching. Here the needy, sick, poor, and old are our trust—from God. Raised in Notre Dame Elementary School in Long Beach, Indiana and La Lumiere RC Boarding School in La Porte, he took to heart this tradition which rises above all expediencies: legal, economic and political, telling us in holy writ and in sacred tradition to care for our neighbors in need. In high school he was an excellent scholar/athlete with five years of Latin and a grounding in French, choir, drama, the school newspaper, and student council. Most likely, he and his teachers among the priests and sisters were steeped in the Catholic tradition's absolute insistence on honoring the poor, workers, the sick, weak, children, "strangers within our gates"—Scripture in sum calls these—the "in as much . . . least of these"—Christ incognito in our midst. As it turns out, we one time immigrants now disdainfully call these neighbors-illegals-freeloaders, leeches, parasites—the old and dying—"the out to pasture"—"we wish you were not here folk." For Judge Roberts, this training trumped demands for political expediency. It now remains to be seen if the "better angels" and religious inculcations of Obama or Romney will also play out toward decency or toward the pressure of money. Will this good homeland of ours find our way toward justice, mercy, care and concern or will all three branches of government remain stalemated while the private sector continues to live frantically by the golden rule that "those who have the gold make the rules"?

We find ourselves today in the important holiday season of Harvest day, Labor day, church rally day, (post-rummage day,) back to school day. It's a hope springs eternal day. As Shakespeare noted—kids with shiny faces and carefully stocked backpacks and lunch boxes "creep off unwillingly to school." The pressing questions of life now change as we frolic from Vivaldi's summer to Auden's autumn–"Are we there yet?" from the back seat of the car—now becomes "When do we start 'Christmas shop till we drop?'"

## Come Labor On

Autumn is resolution and redemption time . . . new beginnings . . . kids off to school . . . limitless horizons . . . life expands.

Where and how does faith come into this pastiche of worldly business? What meaning can we find here? We can start by seeing that in all faiths work is worship. Liturgy (*Leiturgos*)—what we as a faith community are now offering to God—is work offered to The One who alone is worship-worthy—worth our work—this is the One creator/redeemer God who stepped into world history. Just as the history of the world is the history of God, so God-story is our becoming story. John put it this way—to do the work of God is to believe in the One he has sent.

What does this mean? Surely it must mean that God is doing something here and now—in this world—with and through us. God is Emmanuel—God has come into our life to sweep us into God life— God is working. Zion, then Golgotha, then the empty garden tomb is a bulwark—a mighty fortress—a stronghold of care and comfort—a base station from which will proceed redemptive work for the world, lighted path through all darkness, the warehouse of all good and perfect gifts—which come down from the Father of Lights. My teacher at Princeton—Bonhoeffer's friend—Paul Lehmann—said that the key question for faithful folk was—"What is God doing in the world to make and keep human life human?"

The Bible sees the labor of men and the double labor of women as stigmata of the fall, which also means they are windows of freedom and opportunity. All three faiths of Abraham see three besetting sins defacing human life and dishonoring God—our maker and redeemer. The three snares of Baalzebub—that evil one within and among us—are: (1) idolatry -serving "false gods," (2) immorality: wrongful, hurtful treatment of others, and (3) riches. This latter temptation is problematic since we also believe that God prospers the work of our hands. As we work out our salvation with fear and trembling—God is working his purpose out. John's Gospel says that God's working exudes manna in abundance into the world—it is good substance provided for the life of the world. It is meant to be shared and distributed equitably. We misshape it and turn it into mammon by craving it more than God, by grabbing it for ourselves: stealing, hoarding, hiding—while not sharing. Look closely at what is happening with God's abundance poured out into the world as manna.

Economists—who do not like manna/mammon language—have an indicator called per capita GDP. This is the amount of wealth accruing to peoples in the world per year/per person. In Africa, it is $500 per annum—$1.50 per day—in China, it is $5000 per capita/per annum, Singapore $50,000, U.S. $100,000—97% of Americans come in under $250,000, although Sen. Schumer says you can't live in New York for under 1 million, and few small businesses can cash out at $250,000. Three percent of Americans come in at *above 1 million*—this includes a lot of Presbyterians. The top 1% are at 10 to 100 million and above, and they surf in loopholes. We may be seeing for the first time in American history this small sector of millionaire/billionaires able to control elections.

Mr. Adelson says it will be worth $100 million to him to bring down the President—and a frightful multibillion dollar mendacious advertisment now unfolds. In America and abroad, in many places we find an accelerating yawning gap between the very rich and the very poor as the working and the middle class slowly disappear.

Idolatry, injustice, and riches: the snares of Satan are hauling in the storied Jesus fish who spit up coins in the Sea of Galilee—while congressmen skinny-dip and while we neglect the message of the loaves and fishes. Look up our oldest scriptural texts—the Dead Sea Scrolls and the Allepo Codex—fortunately rescued from the rubble of these now beleaguered sites. These treasured scriptures are full of such warnings.

Bring it down to concrete people. In one school in Florida today, thirteen children are homeless, living in cars—and this is typical. They wash up and brush their teeth in a gas station, then off in their car to school—guess we could call it home delivery. One of our colleagues in liturgy today gave me one of my favorite impressionist paintings: Caillebotte—workers scraping and sanding the floors of some some privileged Parisienne—the title of the work is from Matthew (6:34), "sufficient for the day is its own pain."

A few weeks ago we heard that on that day half of the populace nation of India—700 million persons—were without power, without light, without water. That's 10 percent of the world's people. If anyone throws at you the dishonest welfare/work bit these days, just have them cruise the streets of every city in the world at 5 a.m. and see the blacks and browns—poor men and women—going to their work and toil—so much for the myth of privileged white guys still in the pad.

John is talking about this in his treatise on Light, Life, and Bread. Where's God? What's going on? What went wrong in this world destined to be as full of the glory of God as the waters cover the seas? How have we bent it so out of its glorious and generous shape?

Holy text finds a very clear imperative on this matter—here, in this world, God's work entails our work: heal the sick, care for the homeless. It's called neighbor care. Ancient Iran invented "house health," which the Chinese took over as barefoot physicians where someone of every village—a natural nurse—one called to tend to, say 500 people in the parish, knows everyone by name—offering manna, medical, and economic knowledge. Care must be effective—food, jobs, health care, learning, gardening, water access. Only neighbor care can help when lost livelihood can lead to lost health. In America this becomes—diabiesity, no fresh fruit and vegetables—the called ambulance—the ER—the collection agency—the heart attack, exacerbated diabetes—ending in exorbitant national expense—now 17 percent—of that composite GDP we just noted. All because we can't muster the faith and hope to care. When neighbor care disappears—when we are told to fend for ourselves, the world becomes a luxury-liner beached on some drought parched and thirsty land. This is how the Bible describes judgment—a frightening realm where we cease stewarding the world garden and rebel against the divine kingdom of love and reciprocal care and forfeit a flourishing and sufficient creation. By contrast, everywhere we choose to live by neighbor awareness and help—house health, home nursing, house work, house church—here people are upheld from falling through the cracks into the oblivion of anonymity—and the day's pain can be absorbed into God's work —his hand bringing a friend to your hand and his own free and ever-abundant manna.

To bring it home—obviously we're talking about the nineteenth century CE in human history and modernity in the history of God. The era was described most acutely by a prophetic Jew—grandson of rabbis and the son of Protestant believers. Marx and Engels write, "A spectre is haunting Europe, and all the powers of old Europe have formed a holy alliance to impede any remediation of this spectre: Pope and Czar, French radicals and German Police spies. Religion wants to understand we want to change things." Vincent Van Gogh, a contemporary of the German comrades, one who sensitively painted the poor and struggling workers, visited an art exhibit in London devoted to this theme. On one work of the poor huddled in a dark and dangerous London alley, he saw a text from one of his favorite authors—Charles Dickens. It said this: "Dumb, wet, silent horrors. Sphinxes set up against that dead wall and none likely to be at pains to solving them until the general overthrow." Dickens speaks here not of the proletariat revolution but of the God redemption—working out its purpose in the world.

So let us now close and invoke benediction and peace on one another with other words of a great nineteenth-century philosopher/priest—an Anglican who became Catholic and founded the Oxford movement—in part in response to the fact that Catholics better maintained a sacramental solidarity with the poor and didn't give in to the Protestant prosperity gospel. So as we close our labor day meditation on work, world, word and shalom—the words of Cardinal John Henry Newman take on new meaning: "Lord, support us all the day long, until the shadows lengthen and the evening comes, and the busy world is hushed, and the fever of life is over, and our work is done. Then in thy mercy grant us a safe lodging, and a holy rest, and peace at the last. *Amen*."[2]

---

2. Comments: A Labor Day message became the opportunity to consider yet another "intimation of the sacred." Work and love were the two impulses identified by Freud as signature human qualities. Works and fruits are the singular works and fruit of the spirit. My attempt in this message was to elucidate these virtues.

# 11

# Life Together[1]

Emmanuel was in a gang called Mai-Mai. They raped many, including one lovely young woman named Mimi from the village of Gomer. Dirt poor himself, this was Emmanuel's payoff—the spoils of war. Watching women raped and men killed before your eyes is the age-old tactic of making a community lose heart.

That would be the end of the story except that, when all seemed lost, a miracle of love and communion, of grace and forgiveness, entered the anguish and pain. A cross was again to be planted in *pecatta mundi*—the sin of the world. The church and NGOs–our world's best hope for forgiveness and togetherness—got people together in what we call truth and reconciliation ministries.

Emmanuel walked up to Mimi's tiny hut—she spoke quietly and forcefully, "You disgraced me and ruined my life in this community. Now you are my life and you have to take care of me." Emmanuel fell to his knees and begged her forgiveness—he had wronged her with unspeakable violence. She touched his weeping head and forgave him. He then drew a tiny piglet

---

1. Sermon for July 25, 2010, First Presbyterian Church, Evanston, IL. Text: 1 Cor 11:17–26

He was a Congo insurgent—call him Emmanuel—a common name in this land of colonialism and church missions. Our congregation has deep commitments to this torn land.

from beneath his wrap—worth $15—perhaps half a year's wage. She could raise it into a $100 asset.

His gift at the communion altar—you remember—if you are out of peace with your neighbor—first reconcile with your neighbor then bring your gift to the altar—Emmanuel gives his eucharistical gift to her and to Christ, the captain of souls, the head of the table, the face in the Eucharistic altar—the Lord who guides the behavior of both and gives them each to the other in communion—the documentary ends with her walking back home to a new life—leading the piglet with a rope.

The essence of the message of our text today is best expressed by a Lutheran, Dietrich Bonhoeffer, in his work which I often teach—*Life Together* (*Gemeinsames Lebens*). You will recognize the words *Gemeinde*—congregation. This was Luther's translation of Paul's word *Koinonia*—communion. Perhaps you prefer the phrasing of a good Presbyterian. Here's Joe Haroutunian, our Chicago neighbor at McCormick, then University of Chicago, when he writes in his book—God with us. He says this: "The problem of humanity today is that we have lost sight of a 'life together.'" God, writes Haroutunian, communes with us by our communion one with another. Our communion with one another is a sign for God's communion with us.

These are pretty heady statements—if this is so, then communion—like baptism— is a matter of life and death. Perhaps this is why when he was being led to the gallows at Floosenberg and was asked by a friend, "Pastor Bonhoeffer, why are you not afraid?" He answered, "I am not afraid—I have been baptized." Communion is of that import, and that is why it was called in the early church—the *pharmakon ton thanaton*—"the medicine against death."

There's another etymology to koinonia—life together-communion. A sociologist named Toinnes said from earliest human beginnings—there are two kinds of human associations—*Gesellschaft* and *Gemeinschaft*—technical cash transactions—the La Bron James deal—market place transactions of business and commerce—you scratch my back and I'll scratch yours—*Gesellschaft*. Then there are loving, intimate relations—church/family/friendships with God and the other. Human community in God is meant to be communion—*Gemeinde*. Toinnes, of course, got this from the Bible. One of Toinnes students, Martin Buber, put it simply,"We either live as I/It or I/Thou."

But enough academic theology—stick to the text, as Pastor Ray would say—so let's walk together through this text. Let's exegete and exposite this text in some depth. Then we will summarize our findings briefly by noting three insights into communion.

The natural unit here—chosen by Ray and the Worship ministry team—is ten verses—17-26 of 1 Cor 11. Since Paul is a Hellenistic as well as Hebraic writer—and one part can be a roadmap to the next—there is a context in ch. 10 which is essential to understanding ch. 11.

First, note that this is a reality show—it's a real church supper—which at that time was a kind of love feast. In the house churches of Corinth, which like Romans and FPC were right on the tracks bringing both sides —rich and poor together—it was a jungle out there. It's like a picnic or church potluck for which Aunt Bee made her famous chicken pot pie that everyone wants to get to first—like hot dogs on the FPC lawn. Why is it that from the time we are kids we seem to want to get the best for ourselves—this jostling for the best toy, the good seats up front and the choice cuts—this parenesis is the first part of our text and that behavior seems to get worse as we get older.

Sara and I know such churches—we served Second Pres. Chicago. Two groups—exquisitely blended in communion—gay white males and single mom blacks. Then we served Church of Christ Presbyterian—Pan-Asian— classicist *Issi*—refined in faith in the American concentration camps—sixty years ago—and praise-song bopper—*Nisei*—who couldn't even speak Japanese or Korean—yet they blended into a communion song of love. We are thankful when our churches seek to become inclusive communions.

Then in verse 23 our pericope begins a very solemn didache—a sacred, authoritative teaching—an instruction. Patterned on Torah—it is a Jesus rabbinic midrash on Torah—transmitted by Paul—apostle, theologian/ church planter/one who, as much as anyone, is the responsible architect of the Christian church.

Some observations on text and context:

Again it is life and death business—you can die from pandemonium or you can find life. There is some confusion of what is meal and sacred meal. Paul is exasperated when he cries out, "Eat at home and don't be hogs or inconsiderate boors" here. The two meals do belong together but, bottom line, this is no fast-food stop on the way to the beach. Even though these Sunday evening love feasts may occur at someone's back yard barbecue—a house church—this is worship and sacrament. This is the bread/ body life and blood of God—given for sustenance, salvation and life of the world. This Creator God—now clarified for the world in the Son and gifted to the world in the Spirit—is the spirit/life of the world and every living creature—which is everything in creation. Ch. 10—the cup of blessing which we bless, is it not the koinonia of the blood and body of Christ—it is communion with the holy spirit of God. Without this bread and wine, the world and each of us will die. What a mysterious creator and strange creature we have here—said Kazantzakis in *Zorba the Greek*—you put in wine, bread and radishes and out come laughter, sighs, and dreams.

A scan of ch. 10 shows what is really happening in life together, koinonia or communion. We are dealing with the double-barrel sin—the maladies and misdirections of heresy and injustice. These are the twin breaches of the vertical unity or oneness of God and the horizontal way of God—space and time. This of course is the substance of Torah, which is also the Law of Christ or Paul's interesting phrase—the gospel of God (Rom 1:1). You can feel the Decalogue distillation of the biblical way pulsing through chapters 10 and 11.

10:7: don't be idolaters or blasphemers—you sit down to eat and drink then get up to play games.

Breach of Torah is the breaking of our own life lines—again at 10:17 . . . for we being many are one bread and one body for we are all recipients of the one bread.

Union or communion is the gift of the union of God—who is One—with the one world.

So let's bring it home: What is communion, eucharist, mass, the Lord's supper, love feast, dinner with Jesus at the roadside inn near Emmaus? Or in that balcony restaurant—an upper room for Passover Seder? What's going on here, and what does it mean?

Note three movements in this sermon. Communion is: 1. ethereal, 2. earthly, and 3. Eschatological. It is beyond us and here and now. It is down to earth, and it is leading us somewhere new.

Let us lock these in our minds through three of the world's great paintings of the last supper by

Rembrandt, Van Gogh, and Dali.

I.

The early models of communion present what might be called an ethereal understanding. Jewish Passover, Jesus' awesome enactment of that paschal feast—the celebration of the sacrifice of the lambs—all converge into that primal liturgy and moving words—"this is my body." This sublime admixture of heaven and earth is captured in many of the depictions of the Last Supper—especially that of Rembrandt. Something is going on in earth and in eternity. What opens our eyes is what Vincent calls "white light"—*Shekinah*—radiance of the divine presence. Jewish Passover is a theophany—God has made a worldly appearance with a message—angels of death and deliverance—recognizable world antagonists—Pharaoh or later Herod—but always that unseen and uncanny deliverer. In Scripture this is Yaweh and Ben Adam—Son of Man—One who walks silently among us—bringing us together.

Or take another great communion text in the Gospels, one which Pastor Ray walked us through on our focus on Scripture a few weeks ago—the historic travelers from Jerusalem descend down toward Emmaus—dejected, wondering—then they are joined by that ethereal companion, like the crucified one, now at the seaside, now in the upper room, here trodding along the way, like a rabbi opening the scriptural midrash—the parade of texts—explaining why this all happened. Then the stop at the roadside inn and the bread and wine and the breakthrough—he was known to them in the breaking of the bread—then the blind eyes opened and the confused hearts were convinced, and he disappeared into the dark sky—and the remembrance—"did not our hearts burn within us as he taught us along the way?" "Do this in remembrance of me."

There may be something ethereal in these comings and goings, but one thing is certain: we are there and he is there—communion and life—together. Wherever two or three are there, One is in the midst at table's apex—leading out and on—and bread and fish and drink—and bitter herbs and sweet honey.

II.

Communion is also earthy. Van Gogh himself and the world has come to think of *Potato Eaters* as his Last Supper. The poor farmers dug their sustaining breads from the ground—the dirt—the adama—is still on their hands. One scholar of *Potato Eaters* writes: "The sharing of their meager repast alludes to the Eucharist"—remember the bread and fishes in the Gospels—"the ritualistic distribution of the meal acknowledges a holy presence among the humble peasants gathered around the table" (Erickson). Chardin called communion "the Mass upon the earth." For Haroutunian, the communion is rooted in creation and incarnation—in the physical and natural world. These days we feel the call of our stewardship—our solidarity with earth, sea, and sky—with brother sea turtle and sister pelican. Our communion is with flesh and blood—all flesh—says Scripture, all flesh shall see that glory together (Isa 40:5). In 10:26 Paul finds the ultimate meaning of communion in Psalm 24, "the earth is the Lord's and the fullness thereof."

We must cease eating to our own condemnation. Scripture shows us that we wrest our bread from the earth by the sweat of our brow and in the bearing of life and life together—here in the common life the drama of communication and excommunication plays out.

Van Gogh was once asked what really was a religious painting, was it the Garden of Gethsemane with the serene olive groves and the saintly Jesus with a halo? No. He said it was a simple gnarled olive tree standing there for hundreds of years. "People's eyes are the real cathedrals—a human soul, a poor beggar, a street walker." From earth herself, God extends his wayward and onward going in a great circle dance with—bonded and banded—devout and needy people—extended out through all time into all eternity—throughout the whole creation.

### III.

Finally, communion is—as Dali suggests—a journey out into God's new time and place in God's imparted new being and new horizon. It is an eschatological feast . . . Here together we "show forth the Lord's death till he comes." Ultimately communion verges from earth into eternity, where God abides.

In communion, we hold out hands of *Koinonia* fellowship to the other, the stranger, the least of these, even the enemy. Think of the immigrants today in our midst. How urgent now that we offer God's communion to these brothers and sisters who are not only fellow humans but our brothers and sisters in Christ. We must not be tempted aside by those who call for excommunication and extradition.

By now Mimi has raised her piglet and perhaps started a new cottage enterprise. Emmanuel has reentered life as a new reconciled being in Christ—their communion hands out in Congo are joined with ours right now of our people extended across the continents by the Sullivans, the McCauleys, the Rubash eltern, by Caryl Weinberg and the KK Yeos, the McNerneys, Hallidays and Ivaskas—all who follow Jesus, all around the world. Yes, we're the church together. All present company, and by the countless thousands in the communion of Saints past and out into Dali's future horizon—who have been drawn into communion only to be sent out to the ends of the earth. We invite you today to come in, to come together and to move out in this great procession of life together. In the name of the Father who seeds and gathers; the Son who finds and saves and the Spirit who enlivens and grows—the One God who forever fashions human communion—be glory forever. Amen.

# 12

# Joy[1]

"The stars say nothing of the coming of Aslan—nor of peace, nor of joy."[2]

THE HEART OF THE "Intimations of the Sacred" series dealt with what the epistles call "The Gifts of the Spirit"—a set of life principles, virtues or attributes which express in our personal and collective being, "Spirit Life," as opposed to materialistic desire which mitigates against this tableau of behaviors. Joy, peace, love, gentleness and the like turn the world toward the Kingdom of God rather than the Kingdom of Evil, as they become absolute antitheses of sadness, discord, strife, power and the rest.

This biblical tablet of life-patterns follows closely the legal-ethical imperatives of Torah and Hebrew *Halacha*, as well as the Stoic table of virtues borrowed from the enfolding Roman philosophical culture. These pagan virtues were taken over in toto or in modification (see Calvin's reworking of Stoic peace), becoming the ethos of early Christianity.[3]

This particular church worship service dealt with the wide-ranging character of the word "Joy": *Xaris* (Jas 1:2).

We begin with a headline of C. S. Lewis, *Surprised by Joy*—a tribute to his Jewish wife, who died of cancer after they married late in his life. "Joy is

---

1. Sermon preached on Feb. 9, 1992 at Second Pres., Chicago.
2. Lewis, *The Last Battle*, 19.
3. See Meeks, *The Moral World*.

# JOY

a particular kind of unhappiness of grief [remember *A Grief Observed*]. It is the kind we want."

Lewis here expresses his ironic subtlety derived from the biblical letter of James (Jesus' brother). "Count it all joy, when you endure various adversities, knowing that your tested faith produces patience" (Jas 1:2).

The wisdom of the letter to Hebrews is also invoked at this point. "Jesus, for the joy that was set before him endured the cross, despised the shame and sits at the right hand of God (Heb 12:2; see also Phil 2:2).

Those who read and hear these sermons will certainly ask about my "naturalistic" bias. As a Calvinist theologian in the deeper heritage of the theologian Thomas Aquinas, and as a philosophical realist, I do come down firmly on a "natural" metaphysic and morality.

This synthesis, I believe, expresses the finest humanistic wisdom available to humanity. Humanity freed and redeemed is the ultimate theological virtue in a Calvinist perspective. From the view of secular philosophy, behaviors which are rational, justice producing, and conducive to equality, are fulfilling of the noblest aspirations and motivations of persons and communities.

For this reason I have chosen the ideas of William Wordsworth and Samuel Taylor Coleridge and like-minded thinkers in the mystical tradition to provide substance to the notion of "Intimations." This romantic world view is somewhat passé and discredited in the twenty-first century. That is our loss. Enlightenment values themselves are under suspicion.

The amalgam of humanist and theist senses about the phenomenon of joy is expressed throughout the worship service beginning with the beloved cantata "Jesu, Joy of Man's Desiring." Here deepest human yearnings are joined by the noblest theological impulses:

> Jesu, Joy of Man's desiring, Holy wisdom love most bright
> Drawn by thee our souls aspiring, soar to inexpressible light.

Jesus has become the *summum bonum* of Plato and Aristotle
and seconds Hebraic wisdom into one "joyous song."

Scriptural texts proclaim this joy: Psalm 98; John 16:16–26; Hebrews 12:1, 2.

> O sing unto the Lord a new song; for he hath done marvellous things: his right hand, and his holy arm, hath gotten him the victory.

The Lord hath made known his salvation: his righteousness hath he openly shewed in the sight of the heathen.

He hath remembered his mercy and his truth toward the house of Israel: all the ends of the earth have seen the salvation of our God.

Make a joyful noise unto the Lord, all the earth: make a loud noise, and rejoice, and sing praise.

Sing unto the Lord with the harp; with the harp, and the voice of a psalm.

With trumpets and sound of cornet make a joyful noise before the Lord, the King.

Let the sea roar, and the fulness thereof; the world, and they that dwell therein.

Let the floods clap their hands: let the hills be joyful together

Before the Lord; for he cometh to judge the earth: with righteousness shall he judge the world, and the people with equity. (KJV)

Jesus went on to say, "In a little while you will see me no more, and then after a little while you will see me."

At this, some of his disciples said to one another, "What does he mean by saying, 'In a little while you will see me no more, and then after a little while you will see me,' and 'Because I am going to the Father'?" They kept asking, "What does he mean by 'a little while'? We don't understand what he is saying."

Jesus saw that they wanted to ask him about this, so he said to them, "Are you asking one another what I meant when I said, 'In a little while you will see me no more, and then after a little while you will see me'? Very truly I tell you, you will weep and mourn while the world rejoices. You will grieve, but your grief will turn to joy. A woman giving birth to a child has pain because her time has come; but when her baby is born she forgets the anguish because of her joy that a child is born into the world. So with you: Now is your time of grief, but I will see you again and you will rejoice, and no one will take away your joy. In that day you will no longer ask me anything. Very truly I tell you, my Father will give you whatever you ask in my name. Until now you have not asked for anything in my name. Ask and you will receive, and your joy will be complete.

"Though I have been speaking figuratively, a time is coming when I will no longer use this kind of language but will tell you plainly about my Father. In that day you will ask in my name. I am not saying that I will ask the Father on your behalf." (NRSV)

# JOY

> Therefore we also, since we are surrounded by so great a cloud of witnesses, let us lay aside every weight, and the sin which so easily ensnares *us*, and let us run with endurance the race that is set before us, looking unto Jesus, the author and finisher of *our* faith, who for the joy that was set before Him endured the cross, despising the shame, and has sat down at the right hand of the throne of God .(KJV)

The Lord has given victory over the enemies of Israel—a pervasive yet perverse confidence. That the Almighty—the Lord of all peoples—would favor one over another, though natural to human thought and prayer, would seem as incredible as if God favored the Confederacy over the Union in the American Civil War. For the Psalmist, this joy is in deliverance and salvation, release from oppression. It is a celebration of the vindication and righteousness of God. The defeat of Hitler is a saving victory for the German people. Therefore all the earth and creation sing for joy. For the psalmist victory belongs to YAWEH not to the armies of Israel or anyone else. Justice and righteousness belongs to the whole creation and she sings for joy.

As I write this reconstruction of a now lost sermon, a terrible destructive and decimating war has just concluded. It lasted seven weeks. It left most of Palestinian Gaza in rubble. It killed over 2000, mostly innocents, women and children, Arab and Muslim persons. Seventy Israeli soldiers were killed, along with several civilians. Israel was spared greater damage and casualties by an "Iron Dome" donated by the U.S., which obviously did not share the same with the Gazans. Indeed, we supplied most of the planes, rockets, and munitions used against these caged-in, oppressed people.

Though jubilation now occurs on the streets of Tel Aviv and Gaza City, one can only wonder whether we will be back to violence again soon. Tension between Israel and Palestine remains the exacerbating heart of "the war on terrorism" that dominates history from 9/11/01 and before until the bombing of ISIL, which began in force today [9/11/14]. President Obama, now sounding like "a warrior in chief," gives a national address saying that violence doesn't belong to Islam, and Henry Kissinger announcing his new book, *World Order*, is asked if the bombing will end the conflict, and he answers that the warrior impulse is as old as Islam and the "Mahdi" remains one who is "yet to come." Former Secretaries of State Zbignew Brezinski and James Baker resonate over whether ISIS should be challenged to the point of war. There is no "joy" in Mudville: Mighty Casey seems poised to strike out.

And so goes the refrain. Other music in this service reflected on the more pious and spiritual theme of joy: "Jesus, thou joy of loving hearts"[4] and J. S. Bach's "In Thee Is Gladness." I am reminded and reprimanded by an associate in church that my thoughts are partisan and political and the reality of God and Spirit has nothing to do with such matters.

I close this meditation on a personal note. Normally one does not think of death and the cathedral as a matter of joy. This certainly was not the case at Second Pres. when a large gargoyle of stone shook loose from the bell tower façade facing east onto Michigan. It killed a thirty-four-year-old mother of two—Sarah Bean—who lived right adjacent to the great sanctuary, walking by the church on her way to her work as a health care giver twice each day.

When asked by the news media what I, as one of the pastors functioning in the church, thought of the horrific experience, I reminded them of martyrs Jeanne d'Arc at Rouen Cathedral and Jan Hus, who went to the pyre at Constance, who both met their death with the words—"I die with joy at the service of Jesus Christ." Then there was the murder of Thomas Becket, clinging to the sanctuary altar at Canterbury. On more relevant examples, I reminded them of Jesus' teaching on the fallen tower of Siloam that killed eighteen persons, and the fact that more than a hundred masons fell to their death in the 800 years spent building Chartres Cathedral.

Sarah Bean—rest in peace![5]

---

4. Bernard of Clairvaux, 12th century

5. Comments: The original list of "Intimations" was composed of simple one-word items—joy, sorrow, love, joy, peace, snow, power and weakness. Joy and sorrow were found among these archaic sermons.

# 13

# Sorrow[1]

COLIN WAS A DEAR child who was killed, and his father, a coach on the team, was seriously injured. Bruce was wheeled into the sanctuary in his hospital bed, and he lay down front of the chancel next to me and howled in grief as the service unfolded. In a few short years, I would serve at Second Pres., Chicago as interim pastor. The lingering experience of this event expressed in this sermon deeply affected all of the sermons in this book.

I know we should never have left Riverside. As you know, a few weeks ago we left the deep and rich landscape of Riverside for a beach cottage in Hyde Park. To ease the pain of uprooting that we felt as we left Colin, the Andersons, and all of you here in this church and community, we dug up a few lilacs and violets from our big yard on Riverside Road and transplanted them into our postage stamp victory garden on Harper Avenue in Hyde Park. I also planted a lovely crimson clematis—you know that climbing flower that grows big and tall. These all had taken root and had grown for two weeks. But more was not to be. Suddenly and violently something

---

1. The following sermon was given at Riverside Presbyterian Church on May 10, 1990. The occasion was an event—like the conclusion of the last sermon—of overwhelming sorrow and sadness following a tragic accident when a driver blacked out and crashed through the fences of the baseball field killing and injuring several persons, one of whom was a member of the church built by Withers and our relation Calvert Vaux in this historic "first city in a Park in the US" where I served as parish associate. The other boy had been our neighbor on Riverside road.

happened. They all were uprooted and torn down. Tuesday, when I came home from my work on the West Side, they were gone. Something violent had ripped them up and cast them down. A storm—such as we had here in Riverside last night—a wind, maybe a big dog—but these fragile things of beauty were gone. Plants will come again but this uprooting will never leave us. Being left alone is especially awful when it is a son, a brother, a neighbor, a friend.

When Sara and I learned of the whirlwind that had swept across Harrington Park on Saturday afternoon, like most of you we were numb. We hopped in our car and sped to be with Bruce and Penny. How in this placid "City in a Park" could such a maelstrom occur? Just five days ago, the lilacs were bursting with glory and aroma. Neighbors strolled with their children and dogs along our verdant pathways. Well aware of the socioeconomic barriers, the goldfishers plied their lines as they lulled away the hours by the fires across the river from this church. T-ball opening day was here. Then in a split-second:

> I love the dark hours of my being.
> My mind deepens into them.
> There I can find, as in old letters,
> the days of my life, already lived,
> and held like a legend, and understood.
> Then the knowing comes: I can open
> to another life that's wide and timeless.
> So I am sometimes like a tree
> rustling over a gravesite
> and making real the dream
> of the one its living roots
> embrace.[2]

A dream once lost among sorrows and songs. In swept a violent and howling intruder—a wind—a force and in a moment, in what the Bible calls a twinkling of an eye—some of our loveliest and tenderest young flowers were torn up and mercilessly thrown down: Andrew, Timothy and Peter, Bruce and Michael, Jacqueline, Kevin, Andrew and Justin, Holly, Ryan and Colin.

---

2. Rilke, *Rilke's Book of Hours*.

# Sorrow

The pastors and priests of your village have been privileged to walk with you these days of agony. We have shared your grief. We have looked with you into the terrifying eye of the storm. We hope that we will be able to gaze with you, finding that light at the end of the tunnel, that dawn at the end of the dark night. We see with you that hope at the edge of dismay—that God who has been there with us then and now and always—bringing about our good which is his purpose through suffering, death and transfiguration.

Colin was a shaft of light. His lovely smile lit up the night. Sunshine on our shoulder—he made us happy. Unlike Shakespeare's "wining schoolboy creeping like a snail unwillingly to school" (*As You Like It*, act 3) Colin smiled as he skipped off to school—making our day. Penny always had him there a few minutes early, and believe it or not she never had to nudge him out of the car door.

Colin had another smile—one that makes teachers like Penny and Bruce and myself tremble—from his front and center desk in Ms. Horvat's room, he often flashed it; this was the smile that said "You've exhausted this subject—lets move on."

When Penny and Bruce asked me to offer this homily, I asked his school classmates to help me. They made lovely flowers for him on Monday. Here are a few of the petals:

> I like Colin—he would sit with me
> I liked his smile
> His smile made me work
> He shared his crayons with me
> He liked the color purple

For a few moments, let us take the measure of our young friend, what he taught us, and what he continued to show us. If Owen Meany was "the voice" in that uncanny, prophetic novel of John Irving's *A Prayer for Owen Meany*, Colin was the smile. Laughter has two meanings: one earthly, one heavenly. The happy face is rooted in humility and piety.

Laughing and smiling has a down-to-earth quality of humility (root word humus, or "earthy") as much as humorous. Colin was a muddy kind of kid. Whether it was exploring with his friend, Mike Brennan, the secret trails between our houses—or scrounging around in the old coach-house behind his home or just having fun, he was always reveling in life.

The smile or laughter also signals or intimates divinity. There is the sense of irony—the delight when our little orders and rules, systems and schemes—fall apart. The sense of cosmic playfulness, the love of games and sports—mimicking the big game we all play on the stage of life, laughter gently chides what we take too seriously. This is the sense of mischief, of mystery—he was touched by or in touch with something else and his favorite story was *Alice in Wonderland*—need we say more? A kind of magical imagination—in Chesterton's words led him to see a tiger in a pussycat, or helped him transform a lump of cement into gold dust, even an older sister into his best friend.

If we remember his smile, can we ever forget his innocent and kind-hearted glance? The French have a better word for this glance or gaze. *Insouciance*—which means nonchalance, abandonment—is what Colin showed in his glance. This quality is shown in Colin's Ms. Horvat's smile. It was a glance to pass on—the intuition, impatience, the readiness to move on, the sense of running time, transcience. Life's most important lesson is that we are all passing by, here for the moment. Therefore we love, we hope, we fight injustice. We scorn the face of our old adversary, our ancient foe. We know that there is life which is higher, deeper and better than this life. Therefore we know that life is to be valued and lived in its quality not its quantity.

Penny, Bruce, and I have wondered these days whether Colin knew that his mission among us would be so brief. Both parents had a frightful sense that he was "on loan." As the nurse said to the new mother as she handed her her child for the first time—"Here's your baby, hold him for a while." That melancholy unease which we all know regarding life's brevity, terrifies us into faith, hope, and love. It is the secret of our becoming and being human.

There was an evening ritual in the Anderson house. Every night Colin would take the book and read to Bruce until his dad fell asleep, then he tucked him in and went back to his business. As you see, Bruce still carries his bed with him. One story that Colin and Penny struggled with was the King Arthur story of a young boy—Gareth—who feels led away in search for the holy grail and the sword. The child-knight pleads with his mother to let him go. She can't bear to part with him. Colin didn't want to hear this story—when Penny said to him, "Some day you must grow and leave," he said, "No, I never want to leave you, Mom, and I'll never let you die."

"Let this cup pass from me," said the young son in that Garden . . .

Torn between the goodness of life and love here and now and the crimson grail which is our cup as we test and trust the destiny which is ours, we experience the paroxysm of faith in life where falling into death is found to be a falling into greater life. Colin and his family have taught us by their faith that the greatest lesson of life is that transcience renders us tenderhearted and trusting. In rude and cruel fashion, Colin pioneered that journey which we must all follow and we will follow inspired by his courage.

A friend of Colin wrote this letter:

> We had fun together, pillow fights, soccer, basketball and tag, Colin was very bright, he wanted to learn more. He had a good voice, he had a great smile, he was good at piano and good at T-ball. It feels like part of me has vanished. I hope someday when I'm nine I can talk, walk, run, swim, play and see Colin.

Yes, my dear young friend—a part of you has vanished. It's now safe home with him forever. A part of each of us has gone with him—he's okay now, and with God he will nurse us back till we are whole again. Someday—when we're nine, we'll walk, talk, run, swim, play and see him again.

This morning, after last night's storm, a new flower came out in our victory garden; it was Roseum/Rhododendron. It is crimson tinted with blue—I guess you'd call it purple. You know, I think that heaven is crimson tinted with blue.

He always smiled—he was so nice—he liked the color purple. The end of the matter is this—we die unto the Lord, safely held in his grace, therefore, while we live, we live with gusto and generosity—like Colin.

The composer Gustav Mahler knew of the warm love by which we cling to one another, as we do now. He knew of our fear of going out in the rain, he knew of the terrible storm we've been through. He wrote a cycle of songs called *Kindertotenlieder* [Songs on the Death of Children]:

> In this weather, in this shower [Braus], I would never have sent the children out.
> They were dragged out; I was not allowed to say anything against it.
> In this weather, in this storm[Graus], I would never have let the children go out.
> I was afraid it would make them ill, but those were vain thoughts.
> In this weather, in this awful storm [Saus], I would never have let the children go out.
> I was afraid that they would die tomorrow, but there is nothing to do about that now.

In this weather, in this awfulness, I would never have sent the children out.

They were dragged out; I was not allowed to say anything against it.

In this weather, in this storm, in this shower, they are resting.

resting as if they were at home with mother. Frightened no more by storms. Watched over by God's hand, they are resting as if they were at home with mother.[3]

---

3. Commentary: We've included this eulogy for Colin as an example of an "Intimation" of the sacred, accessible as sorrow becomes a sacrament—confronting us with the Holy. Sorrow does not always lead to redemption—to joy in the morning. Sorrow can become chronic, pathological and demonic. That Jesus extolled sorrow in the Beatitudes: "Blessed are those who mourn—they will be comforted" (Matt 5:4) and in John's Gospel, "Your sorrow will be turned to joy" (16:20), shows the deeper mystery where grief and sorrow discloses its secret as we bear it with one another.

# 14

# Lion Power

THIS SERMON HAS NEVER been preached, though it is in every message I have ever spoken. It draws on texts across the seven volumes of C. S. Lewis' Chronicles of Narnia. When President Kennedy was killed in Dallas in 1963, our preacher in Pittsburgh at the grief wake said, "Today President Kennedy died in Dallas, C. S. Lewis died in Cambridge, England, and an unknown child died in Calcutta, India—In the eyes of God, all were the same."

Lewis sternly resisted literalizing his animal stories, but his best theology, his doctrine of God, man, and the world, is embedded in the story of the Lion King in the seven children's books. Walk with me as we scour these seven pieces to find "Jack's" view of God and the greater sacred reality. We will do this by etching the image of the Lion, as did the Byzantines on the gates of Venice.

## BOOK 1: *THE MAGICIAN'S NEPHEW*

The story begins with magic, on earth with Uncle Andrew and at the membrane to beyond in Narnia with the witch. Both creation in the world and in supernature is enchanted. As G. K. Chesterton, J. R. R. Tolkien, Lewis Carroll, and others of the Inklings showed, all reality is God-suffused. This enchantment, best conveyed in stories, is C. S. Lewis' theological starting point.

Enter Aslan—the Lion King.

He is restlessly wandering back and forth on the empty land, singing a new song, creating cosmos from the chaos and precariousness of the raw material that will form creation.

"The lion was pacing to and fro about that empty land and singing his new song. It was softer and more lilting than the song by which he had called up the stars and the sun; a gentle rippling music. And as he walked and sang the valley grew green with grass. It spread out from the lion like a pool. It ran up the sides of the little hills like a wave. In a few minutes it was creeping up the lower slopes of the distant mountains, making that young world every moment softer."[1]

One cannot read C. S. Lewis' fictional material, even the substantive material (e.g., *Mere Christianity*) and miss the point that he is a biblically grounded thinker and apologist. One feels Genesis with its dual message, tracing the emergence of the good and the evil. One feels the temptation, the thrilling and terrible freedom—then the ongoing saga of damnation and redemption.

Lewis frequently owns that he subscribes to this biblical narrative as it is mediated through Plato. The neoplatonic rendition of Jewish/Christian Scripture and revelation becomes part and parcel of Christian tradition and Lewis anchors his teaching at this point. Such a pathway of interpretation lends itself to a literary and idealistic approach such as that employed by the Oxford/Cambridge master. For Platonism creation is ephemeral—for Lewis it is concrete, finding truth best in mythic stories. Creation flows from the "lion's head," which is the "mind of God." Creation thus becomes a matter of faith. Karl Barth, we recall, found the core and essence of what we have of God to be the Living, Written, and Preached word mediated into our minds and lives by the disciplines of exegesis, dogmatics, and homiletics.

The lion then assembled all the creatures into a grand circle still singing, still calling all into being, still creating *Imago dei/Vox dei*—likeness and voice—reminding one of the biblical music of the spheres.

"The lion, whose eyes never blinked, stared at the animals—as if he were going to burn them up . . . his warm breath seemed to sway all the beasts . . . Narnia, Narnia, Narnia, he said awake. Love. Think. Speak. Be walking trees. Be talking beasts. Be divine waters. Hail Aslan (resounds the

---

1. Lewis, *Magician's Nephew*, 112.

creation), We hear and obey. We are awake. We love. We think. We speak. We know."² Creation is spoken into being.

The primal harmony of the creation—fresh, pristine and good—was despoiled in the view of C. S. Lewis. The wicked witch is Lewis' version of what scripture calls "Hosatan" (Job) or what the broader neoplatonic biblical heritage places within the dialectics of Gog and Magog, Christ and Antichrist.

Digory, the son of Adam, whose mother is critically sick, challenges Aslan on the complicating presence of the witch, one to whom we must remember in Lewis' theology and view of evil is given over Aslan's life. The Lion asks Digory why he brought the witch to Narnia. The son of Adam (of Man) confesses—"I brought her, Aslan." For what purpose the Lion asks his human offspring. "I wanted to get her out of my own world back into her own," Digory replies. "I thought I was taking her back to her own place."³

Aslan continues his *Schopfungsrede* (preaching on the creation):

"You see friends that before the new, clean world I gave you is seven hours old, a force of evil has already entered it; waked and brought hither by this son of Adam . . . But do not be cast down evil will come of that evil but it is still a long way off and I will see to it that the worst falls upon myself . . . as Adam's race has done the harm, Adam's race shall help to heal it."⁴

Lewis is not at all subtle and symbolic at this point. This is dead-earnest Christian theology. This is Genesis. This is the *protoevangelium*—the announcement of the catastrophic fall and the counter of redemption. "Since by man came death by man came also the resurrection of the dead. As in Adam all die so in Christ (the second Adam) shall all be made alive" (1 Cor 15).

Now even in volume 1 of Narnia we learn that Aslan himself will bear the primal curse and be put to death. Rather than running in fear when children hear this part of the story they shudder and cry out to mom—"Read on!"

As we will explore in the concluding sermons of this series, The Lion represents the polar aspects of the being of the one true God. C. S. Lewis explores this in the Narnian chronicles as the God figure Aslan combines both surpassing power and sympathetic weakness. In vol. 1—*The Magician's Nephew*—he paints narratively the creator and new creator as one

2. Ibid., 126–27.
3. Ibid., 146.
4. Ibid., 148.

who is also a vulnerable creature. Aslan will be tied down and killed and for now—like the crucified One—he is sympathetic with our deepest pain.

Digory—the son of Adam—pleads with the Lion searching for the virtue of his power to heal his sick mother:

"But please, please, won't you—can't you give me something that will cure mother?" In Christian nomenclature he is pleading for the *pharmacon tou theou*, the medicine against death. Lewis continues, "Up till then he had been looking at the Lion's great feet and the huge claws on them; now in his despair he looked up at his face. What he saw surprised him as much as anything in his whole life. For the tawny face was bent down near his own and (wonder of wonders) great shining tears stood in the Lion's eyes. They were such big, bright tears compared with Digory's own . . . 'My son, my son,' said Aslan. 'I know grief is great. Only you and I in this land know that yet. Let us be good to one another . . . a tree in the garden of Narnia will protect [your mother].'"[5]

## SUM OF THE MATTER—*EDAKRUSEN O IASUN*—JESUS WEPT—JOHN 11:35.

Book 1 concludes its theological portrait of the reality of God in creation through the picture of Aslan with explication of the healing tree of life with the silver apples in the paradise garden.

"Son of Adam," said Aslan "You have sown well and you Narnians, let it be your first care to guard this tree, for it is your shield. The witch of whom I told you has fled far away into the North of the world; she will live on there, growing stronger in dark Magic. But while that tree flourishes she will never come down into Narnia."[6]

The stage is set for the unfolding drama of redemption in creation.

## BOOK 2: *THE LION, THE WITCH AND THE WARDROBE*

Volume 2 is the vastly popular *The Lion, the Witch and the Wardrobe*. This story is pivotal to Lewis' portrait of Aslan the Lion and his continuing development of a theology of God and the world. The Oxford/Cambridge professor of Medieval Literature opens this book by introducing a professor

5. Ibid., 54.
6. Ibid., 189.

who seems to teach philosophy, theology, logic and ethics. He is a tutor to the earthlings—sons of Adam—who are penetrating the membrane between earth (London) and the beyond, Narnia. He warns these mariners of the importance of veracity and of the necessity of imagination.

Lucy has glimpsed hints or intimations of another world through the simple mystery of the wardrobe, the entry into another realm . . . one eternal yet somehow tangential to our own domestic reality. They think she is lying.

"[T]his all couldn't be true all this about the wood and the Faun," the playmates say, even though we know Lucy to be an honest friend. The Socratic wisdom of the professor retorts, "This is more than I know . . . and a charge of lying against someone you have always found truthful is a very serious thing."

"We thought that she was lying or that there was something more serious wrong with Lucy."

"Madness you mean," retorts the Professor.

Then in a passage about logic—one which C. S. Lewis often uses about truthfulness (e.g., in *Miracles, Mere Christianity*, etc)—"There are only 3 possibilities. Either your sister is telling lies, or she is mad or she is telling the truth."[7] The Professor teaches his class not only in ethics and logic but in his openness to mystery beyond supposed and assumed reality. With this epistemological morass resolved, at least for the moment the children confront the question—"Who is Aslan?"[8]

Lewis responds to his own question with two rhymes:

> Wrong will be right, when Aslan comes in sight,
> At the sound of his roar, sorrows will be no more,
> When he bares his teeth, winter meets its death,
> And when he shakes his mane, we shall have spring again.
>
> When Adam's flesh and Adam's bone
> Sits at Cair Paravel in throne,
> The evil time will be over and done.[9]

The disarming and defanging of evil occupies the rest of vol. 2. This is accomplished by Aslan's saving presence and redemptive plan. Much of the

---

7. *The Lion, The Witch*, 52.
8. Ibid., 85.
9. Ibid., 85, 87.

proleptic plan is already put into motion and Aslan discloses its secret at the end of *The Lion, the Witch and the Wardrobe*.

"At last they [the animals and Adam's children] heard Aslan's voice. "You can all come back," he said. "I have settled the matter. She [the Witch] has renounced the claim on your brother's blood."

As she withdraws, vanquished for the moment, she asks, "How do I know that this promise will be kept?"

"'Haa-a-arrh!' roared Aslan, half rising from his throne; and his great mouth opened wider and wider and the roar grew louder and louder, and the Witch, after staring for a moment with her lips wide apart, picked up her skirts and fairly ran for her life."[10]

The die is cast. The metaphysical deal has been struck. The queen has received her frightful and so costly bargain and now the transaction must be fulfilled.

"He that spared not His only Son, but gave him up for us all, how will he not freely give us all things in Him" (Rom 8:32).

Volume 3, *The Horse and His Boy*, furthers the God saga with a wilderness journey (Moses?) and a battle. Aslan the Lion for the most part is incognito. *Deus Incognito* is a deep tradition in the scriptural heritage. *Deus Absconditas*. Likewise is the *Ego Eimi*: "I Am that Am," "The Burning Bush," or with Jesus the "When did we see you hungry and feed you?" Though everpresent the Lion does make one appearance.

In the Golden Age of Narnia Peter is the High King and his brother and two sisters are Kings and Queens under him. Shasta, the son of a poor fisherman and his horse are the principal characters. These two personages also have prominent place in biblical heritage. Humble beginnings of persons and humble and noble steeds are visible from Genesis to Revelation. David appears on donkey and horse. Jesus rides into Jerusalem on a donkey—indeed the foal of a donkey, and in Revelation we envision the four horsemen of the apocalypse—ultimately the white Christ horse.

We recall from earlier in the Chronicles that the Narnia animals are given the gift of image and speech.

"The happy land of Narnia" (now with the gift of gab) is where I learned to speak.— Narnia of the heathery mountains and the Thymy downs (spicy speech/so humorous), Narnia of the many rivers, the plashy glens, the mossy caverns and the deep forests ringing with the hammers of dwarfs. Oh the sweet air of Narnia!—his speech ended with a whinny

---

10. Ibid., 158.

that sounded like a sigh."[11] Never have the animals been so eradiate as they become by the pen of "Jack."

This section of the Narnia introduces for the first time the issue of heresy. We now meet alien peoples and gods. Tashbaan, Tisroc and the pseudogod Tash cross the stage. The strangers are not British-Americans—they appear Persian, foreign, even Muslim. From the dawn of monotheism the entre of aliens, others and "other gods" is placed in sharp relief for good and bad. C. S. Lewis with his rich palette is calling on the great God of the whole world in all of its rainbow colors and variety of creatures. This variety—even of faiths—of course, raises certain difficulties. Do "many gods"refute the validity of the One God in One world for One Humanity and One Creation? Can the unity of God not end up in vilification, anathematizing others, even overt violence. Too often monotheists end up eliminating and eradicating any and all "others." Conversely the One God of all makes all One—not by diminishing but by reason of their diversity.

The desert/wilderness sojourn of Shasta finds him one night among the tombs. Like the New Testament incident where lepers were forced to live among the tombs and declare themselves as unclean (separate). Such imposed exile and isolation of lepers is related to the just discussed matter of prejudicial rejection of some who are different. We wish to separate ourselves from those with different views on sexual orientation, those of different racial or economic status. Ultimately this rejection all devolves back on some sense of superiority or contamination. Lewis is a prophetic theological figure preaching—through his emissaries like Aslan—the grand providential design of all creation—human, animal, natural, supernatural, earthly, alien—all enraptured in a joyous yet challenging drama of creation.

The barbarous (barbarian) countries like the Tisroc and Tashban—like the uncivilized non-faith proponents of ISIL—now being bombed from their strongholds in Syria and Iraq by a Christian and Sunni Muslim (Arab) coalition in September of 2014, even as the UN meets—are treated as the enemies of creation and humanity.

## BOOK 3: *THE HORSE AND HIS BOY*

As battle nears in Narnia 3 (*The Horse and His Boy*), Lewis speaks of dislodging an evil power holding the world in her (the queen of evil) grip. The Vizier and the Prince speak, "little barbarian countries like ours call

11. Ibid., 158.

themselves free—are hateful to the gods . . . know this, O enlightened Prince, until this year when your exaulted father began his salutatory and unending reign—the land of Narnia was covered with ice and snow and was ruled over by a powerful enchantress."

"I know [the prince replies] that the enchantress is dead—and the ice and snow have vanished so that Narnia is now wholesome . . ."[12]

As I write these reflections on the theological meanings of the Lion in the Chronicles of Narnia, a strange confluence of events shakes the world. Even as the U.N. ponders withdrawing or expansion of the Arctic ice pack along with the effects of global warming—nothing less than our own ice-queen—the world also ponders other dimensions of natural and human harm and destruction in the world—war in the ancient biblical lands of Mesopotamia.

Volume 3 ends with one of the most moving and descriptive passages on Aslan the Lion.

> Shasta, the boy did not know the true stories about Aslan, the great lion, the son of the Emperor—over Sea, the King above all High Kings in Narnia. But after one glance at the lion's face he slipped out of the saddle and fell at its feet. He couldn't say anything, and he knew he needn't say anything.
>
> The High King above all kings stooped towards him. Its mane, and some strange and solemn perfume that hung about the mane, was all round him. It touched his forehead with its tongue. He lifted his face and their eyes met. Then instantly the pale brightness of the mist and the fiery brightness of the Lion rolled themselves together into a swirling glory and gathered themselves up and disappeared. He was alone with the horse on a grassy hillside under a blue sky. And there were birds singing.[13]

Isaiah 6:

> In the year that king Uzziah died I saw also the Lord sitting upon a throne, high and lifted up, and his train filled the temple
> Then said I, Woe is me! for I am undone; because I am a man of unclean lips, and I dwell in the midst of a people of unclean lips: for mine eyes have seen the King, the Lord of hosts.
> Then flew one of the seraphims unto me, having a live coal in his hand, which he had taken with the tongs from off the altar:

---

12. Lewis, *The Horse and His Boy*, 108.
13. Ibid., 160.

And he laid it upon my mouth, and said, Lo, this hath touched thy lips; and thine iniquity is taken away, and thy sin purged.
Also I heard the voice of the Lord...

## BOOK 4: *PRINCE CASPIAN*

Book 4 of The Chronicles elaborates the story of Prince Caspian (and of Aslan).

"A circle of grass as smooth as a lawn with dark trees dancing all round it met (Lucy) her eyes. And then—oh joy! For He was there: the huge Lion, shining white in the moonlight, with his huge black shadow underneath him ... the next thing she knew was that she was kissing him and putting her arms as far round his neck as she could and burying her face in the beautiful rich silkiness of his mane.

"Aslan, Aslan. Dear Aslan, sobbed Lucy. At last."

The great beast rolled over on his side so that Lucy fell, half sitting and half lying between his front paws. He bent forward and just touched her nose with his tongue. His warm breath came all round her. She gazed up into the large wise face.

"Welcome child," he said.

"Aslan," said Lucy, "you're bigger."

"That is because you are older, little one."

"... every year you grow, you will find me bigger."

From somewhere deep inside Aslan's body there came the faintest suggestion of a growl.

" I couldn't have left the others and come up to you alone, how could I?"

"You must all get up and follow me—what will happen? There is only one way of finding out."

He got up and walked with stately, noiseless paces back to the belt of the dancing trees.

I'll walk with God from this day on. His helping hand I'll lean upon. I'll pray to Him, each day to him and He'll hear the words that I say—I'll walk with God.[14]

The Shofar sounds.

It is *Ros Hasha'nah*.

14. Sigmund Romberg, *The Student Prince*, 1952.

## Second Sermons

The New Year.

The first day of the world.

Cast me not away from your presence and take not your holy spirit from me.

"Look," Edmund said in great excitement." Look! What's that shadow crawling down in front of us ?"

"It's his shadow, "said Lucy

"Where is he?" said Edmund

"Within his shadow of course."

The long gentle slope (heather and grass and a few very big rocks that shone white in the moonlight) stretched up to where it vanished in a glimmer of trees about half a mile away. She knew it. It was the hill of the Stone Table.[15]

Lewis concludes: As for power, do not the stories say that the Witch defeated Aslan, and bound him and killed him on that very stone which is over there just beyond the light?

But they also say that he came to life again.[16]

"Auntie's very ill." The little girl said, "She's going to die." Then Aslan went to go in at the door of the cottage, but it was too small for him. He pushed his shoulders and full body through and lifted up the whole house and it fell backwards and apart. The old woman was at death's door. She opened her eyes and saw the bright, hairy head of the lion staring into her face, she did not scream or faint. "Oh Aslan! I knew it was true. I've been waiting for you all my life. Have you come to take me away?" "Yes, dearest," said Aslan. "But not the long journey yet."

Jesus rose up out of the synagogue and entered into Peter's house. His wife's mother was taken with a great fever, and they besought him for her.

And he stood over her and rebuked the fever and it left her and immediately she arose and ministered unto them. [Luke 4: 38,39]

## BOOK 5—*THE VOYAGE OF THE DAWN TREADER*

The Apostle Paul often boarded ships headed for the far extremes of the Roman world. The journies of Jonah to dangerous climes and places is recalled. Today after bombings in the Middle East by ISIL—a pseudo-voyager to pure religion—Mosul, the church of Jonah, lies in rubble. The psalmist

---

15. Lewis, *Prince Caspian*, 135-47.

16. Ibid., 162, 163.

## Lion Power

and prophets speak of the East and West, North and South—distant points which still entertain the divine presence and leading. Such uttermost parts—even under the world—are not exempt of his presence (Ps 103).

The journey or voyage is a metaphorical way of speaking of the story of God and humanity in a dynamic way. C. S. Lewis is a particularly cogent master of the ontological and temporal aspects of metaphysical reality. *Treader* is on the way to the last boundary and the last battle of the cosmic creation. It centers again in the actual and hidden presence of the One from whom the cosmos comes and in whom it coheres (Colossians). As C. S. Lewis says in the books introduction to Aslan,

"The King, Lord of the whole wood, and son of the Emperor across the Sea. Aslan is the Lion, the great Lion. He comes and goes as and when he pleases; He comes to overthrow the witch and save Narnia."[17]

In the great time warp, "Lucy, Peter and Susan had been Kings and Queens in Narnia long before his time." If you spent a hundred years in Narnia, you would still come back to our world at the very same hour of the very same day on which you left.[18]

A thousand years in thy sight are as yesterday when it is past, as a watch in the night (Ps 90:3).

The voyage of the Dawn Treader is the search for the "dawn" after a seeming endless night of darkness. It is a journey East—for Aslan lives in the East—the far East. Faith is always thought to arise in the orient—the land of the rising sun. The sun sets in the occident—the West—the *Abenlandes*—the lands of the setting sun. All of the faiths purport to have originated in the East. In Asia, the religions of India—Buddhism and Hinduism. Judaism, Christianty and Islam all search the East for their freshness, newness and vitality. The West is a place of decadence, oldness—where things burn out.

Reepicheep, the mouse, speaks for the inner meaning of the voyager's quest: "Why should we not come to the very eastern end of the world? What might we find there? I expect to find Aslan's own country. It is always from the East, across the sea that the lion comes to us."[19]

C. S. Lewis reflects on this symbolic passage with a rhyme through the wise speech of the mouse:

Where sky and water meet,

17. Lewis, *Voyage of the Dawn Treader*, 7.
18. Ibid., 13.
19. Ibid., 21.

> Where the waves grow sweet,
> Doubt not, Reepicheep,
> To find all you seek,
> There is the utter East.[20]

## DARKNESS AND FAITH

"If I say surely darkness shall cover me; even the night shall be light about me . . . Darkness and Light are both alike to Thee" (Ps 139: 10–12).

C. S. Lewis is one of the noble company of those who struggle with faith including Augustine, Luther, Calvin, Mother Teresa, and others. Augustine wrote, "Despair not, one of the thieves was spared. Presume not, one of the thieves was not." This word headlined the recent film *Calvary*.

It is in the West where the purity of Eastern desert faith is put to the test. Artists recourse to the Pacific Islands and writers, poets and philosophers travel to India or Sinai.

On the back alleys of Calcutta, Mother Teresa found peace and light with the poor but her inner modern soul found darkness and torments. In her 1953 diaries she pleaded for a recovery of the sense of God to dispel the gloom. "Please pray specifically for me that I may not spoil His Work and that our Lord may show Himself—for there is such terrible darkness within me as if everything was dead."

Such cleansing is confronted by C. S. Lewis in book 5. Eustace, a cousin of the siblings who are the Kings and Queens of Narnia—the children of Adam—reports of when he had been transformed into a dragon as they sail on the voyage of the Dawn Treader.

> Following the Lion up into the mountains there was moonlight over and round the Lion wherever we went. On top of the mountain there was a garden with trees and fruit and in the middle a great well.
>
> I went to dive in but the Lion told me that I must undress first. He scraped off his skin and scales only to find underneath skin after skin. Finally the Lion said, "I must undress you." And Eustace could only think of the big, sharp claws.
>
> The very first tear that he made was so deep that I thought it had gone right into my heart. And when he began pulling the skin

---

20. Ibid., 22.

off, it hurt more than anything I've ever felt... then he caught hold of me and threw me into the water. I was a boy again.

Wash me and I shall be whiter than snow... (Ps 51).
"I think you've seen Aslan," said Edmund. "Who is Aslan? Do you know him? Well he knows me."[21]

Biblical thought and ritual ponders the deep mysteries of dirty and shoddy clothing and of shedding these for new being in washing and baptism.

Toward the end of vol. 5, Lewis concludes drawing from Coleridge's *The Rime of the Ancient Mariner*. This pure white bird traced day and night the voyage. Then he is gone. "So all afternoon with great joy they sailed southeast with a fair wind. But nobody noticed when the albatross had disappeared."[22] Another trailer and hound of heaven—the One ubiquitous presence.

## BOOK 6—*THE SILVER CHAIR*

In book 6—*The Silver Chair*—Prince Rilian escapes from the Emerald Witches' underground kingdom. The incident of the sailing of King Caspian now culminates with a sojourn of the Kings and Queens in the wilderness and wastelands before the final destination is reached. The exploration and detailed elaboration of the underworld prepares for the conclusion of the Chronicles in the "Last Battle" and the final conquest of evil by Aslan in Narnia.

## THE WATER OF LIFE

C. S. Lewis is always invoking the Johannine metaphors of God: Bread, Light, Water, and the like. Aslan's early words in *The Silver Chair* center here.

Moving on the journey, Jill is thirsty. A voice comes "If you are thirsty, you may drink." The voice is not the teacher at the well with the Samaritan woman; it is Aslan.

"Are you not thirsty?" said the Lion.
"I'm dying of thirst," said Jill.

21. Ibid., 117.
22. Ibid., 203.

"Then drink," said the Lion.

"I daren't come and drink," said Jill.

"Then you will die of thirst," said the Lion.

"O dear!" said Jill, coming another step nearer. "I suppose I must go and look for another stream then."

"There is no other stream," said the Lion.[23]

Lewis is here exercising his "one source and one only" mode of the transmitted life of God theology. God is being characterized in this moving metaphor which as Lewis knows well is carried through from the Old Testament to the New.

The life of God is imparted into the world through people. Can God operate in the world apart from humans? Of course, as in the pre-human moments of the creation. But God chooses to redeem and remedy the world with people—*Tikkun Olam*.

The direction and origin is also clear in the same passage. "You would not have called to me unless I had been calling to you," said the lion.[24]

An important section follows in vol. 6 as the Chronicles move toward culmination. This section confirms my thesis in this second sermon that Lewis is seeking in Narnia to exposit a full-orbed view of biblical theology and justice.

This section of the *Silver Chair* outlines the template of that overview as it sets forth a set of commands about how to negotiate the life journey and of how to live creatively and responsively in Narnia. The first plan involves signposts on the journey—greeting a friend, journeying to the North, etc. The overarching point here is that life with God is oriented and orienting.

More important is the final admonition "say the signs day and night" and "I give you a warning—Here on the mountain I have spoken to you clearly. I will not often do so down in Narnia. Here on the mountain the air is clear and your mind is clear; as you drop down into Narnia the air will thicken."[25]

C. S. Lewis is making clear—here in the clear air and with clear mind— that he is a Jewish or messianic Christian. The passage evokes images of Sinai or the Beatitudes mountain. It also is fully deuteronomic: "I have set before you life and death—choose life" (Deut 30:19).

Lewis ends this penultimate book with moving summarial images:

---

23. Lewis, *The Silver Chair*, 16–18.
24. Ibid., 19.
25. Ibid., 21.

## Lion Power

King Caspian had died and lay like Das Rheingold at the glistening floor of the river. All three of the children, Kings and Queens, "stood and wept. Even the lion wept: great Lion tears, each tear more precious than the earth would be if it was a single solid diamond."

"Son of Adam," said Aslan, "Go into that thicket and pluck the thorn that you will find there . . . (it was a foot long and as sharp as a rapier)—Drive it into my paw Son of Adam. Eustace set his teeth and drove the thorn into the Lion's pad—and the dead king (Caspian) began to change."[26]

## BOOK 7—*THE LAST BATTLE*

*The Last Battle* won the Carnegie Medal for excellence in children's literature. The watchword for vol. 7 and the whole Chronicles is simple: "The Good Lion was the one whose blood saved all Narnia."[27] Narnia is earth and earth is heaven in Lewis' eschatological cosmology: "all worlds draw to an end, except Aslan's own country."[28]

The final book begins with a section on the reality and veracity of pseudogods—in this case the impersonator god Tash. It proceeds to a treatise on the "shadowlands" where virtual and authentic humanity is declared. Finally, in one of the most hauntingly beautiful sections of the entire Chronicles, Lewis speaks of his overlapping worlds of Narnia, London, and all other worlds in this multidimensional cosmos.

"The ape jumped up and spat on the lamb. Tash is only another name for Aslan."[29] The old deceiver is alive and well as Aslan begins the final undertaking of bringing Tikkun (repair) to Narnia. If the world that God the creator/redeemer has fashioned under the will, voice and breath of Aslan—this hardy deputy—falsehood must be exposed and truth established by this ambassador in association with humanity and the rest of creaturedom.

The night must fall and the necessary last battle must be fought. Numerous events transpire before human existence is rendered finally ready and animality is perfected. In the metaphor "shadowlands" (remember the biographical film of "Jack" and Joy) the misty present day obscurities and enigmas (like disease and death) must be brought into submission.

---

26. Ibid., 211, 212.
27. Lewis, *The Last Battle*, 42.
28. Ibid., 111.
29. Ibid., 40.

## Second Sermons

"The last enemy to be destroyed is death" (1 Cor 15). "[U]ntil He has put all enemies under His footstool" (Ps 110:1; Matt 22:44).

Human fulfillment and renewal is central to the drama of redemption and expansion which unfolds as book 7 proceeds toward conclusion.

> "I see," Lucy said at last, "This garden is like a stable. It is far bigger inside than it was outside."
>
> "Of course, Daughter of Eve," said the Faun, "the further up and further in you go, the bigger everything gets. The inside is larger than the outside."
>
> Lucy looked hard at the garden and saw that it was not really a garden but a whole world, with its own rivers and woods and sea and mountains. But they were not strange: she knew them all.[30]

The animal kingdom is a pinnacle of the divine creation—

"the very first person whom Aslan called to him was Puzzle the donkey."[31]

The ending of the Chronicle is full of tension yet with resolution.

> "You do not yet look so happy as I mean you to be," said Aslan.
>
> Lucy said, "We're so afraid of being sent away, Aslan. And you have sent us back into our own world so often."
>
> "No fear of that,," said Aslan. "Have you not guessed?"
>
> Their hearts leaped and a wild hope rose within them.
>
> "There was a real railway accident," said Aslan softly. "Your father and mother and all of you are—as you used to call it in the Shadowlands—dead. The term is over: the holidays have begun. The dream is ended: this is the morning."
>
> And as He spoke He no longer looked to them like a lion; but the things that began to happen after that were so great and beautiful that I cannot write them. Now at last they were beginning Chapter One of the Great Story which no one on Earth has read: which goes on forever.[32]

---

30. Ibid., 224.

31. Ibid., 227.

32. Comments: C. S. Lewis is my mentor and model-stylist. I hope now having outlived him for a decade to learn to write (preach) like him. He bridges the theological and the commonplace. chasm (liberal/conservative) which aggravates the church in this world so much that it invalidates any meaningful witness. Proofs of the faith do not work. Doctrinal systems are not helpful. Faith must be put into narrative as "Jack "showed us.

# 15

# That Day/Wondrous Love[1]

AFTER THE RADIANCE OF Christmastide and the winter light of Epiphany, we have settled into the everafter glow of ordinary time. While to winter's coldness are added the conundrums of fires and floods pressing our cabin fever toward agitation, we patiently wait it out as word proceeds to work in the world. Our only repose it seems to this bleak mid-winter was another unbearable Super Bowl. Maybe our '96–97 Bulls have charged up your batteries, especially the three superheroes: Superman, Batman and Rodman. Closer meditation to the time at hand discloses a season far from boring—one liturgically and theologically vibrant. The Word which God sent has gone out into all the world. Now like growing seed or latent roots, it is gathering strength; never to return empty (but accomplishing its mission). This active and living Word—the veritable music of the spheres—sings a stirring duet. The two voices: "That Day" and "Wondrous Love." Like Richard Tucker and Robert Merrill's "Temple Saint" duet from Bizet's *Pearl Fishers* or Kathleen Battle and Jessye Norman's *Lakmé*—a poignant and expectant song has gone out into all the world. "That day . . . wondrous love."

>Like dueling trumpets on old Shechem's mountain of covenant renewal.
>Like the dual thrones of Psalm 89:

---

1. Sermon delivered at Garrett Evangelical Theological Seminary Chapel, Spring,1996, earlier version at Second Pres. Isaiah 58 and Matthew 5.

> Two energies pulsate through the cosmos
> The entropy of "that day"
> The negentropy of "wondrous love"
> The weighty matter and drag of sin and law converted by the vulnerable yet
> highly charged matter of grace

## THAT DAY—WONDROUS LOVE

Let us reflect for a moment on this graceful dialogue.

It is now two years since I joined this august company and offered my first sermon. If I've learned anything from the giants who walk these hallowed halls it would be this:

The essence of Torah and Gospel, of prophecy and parenesis, of wisdom and writings—is the complementary tension of judgment and mercy, sedek and hesed, that day and wondrous love. Two pictures appear on the horizon of world history. They depict these two voices: ominous El Greco skies over Toledo verge back toward Christ's Calvary and a glorious sun rises yet over Lake Michigan, piercing the dark winter sky refracted through Tiffany's resplendent ascension window at Second Presbyterian. The Bible sings this duet against this panorama as scripture speaks incessantly of "that day" and "wondrous love."

Our service today enacts the oscillation of this alpha and omega wave: It is there on Doug Anderson's introit from George Herbert and Ralph Vaughan Williams:

> Such a way as gives us breath,
> Such a truth as ends all strife,
> Such a life as killeth death,
> That day/wondrous love.

It is there in our processional hymn recalling fire and Timothy:

> I know not why God's "wondrous grace" to me he has made known. But I know whom I believe and am persuaded that he is able to keep that which I've committed unto him against "that day."

It is there in Doug's song with the choir from Faure's *Requiem*:

> Dies Irae—day of wrath—"that day"
> libera me—deliver me—"wondrous love."

## That Day/Wondrous Love

And by the way, Aretha Franklin, that "deliver me" is not Domino's Pizza. You should have listened to your preacher dad or your friend Lou Rawls, before you did that ad. Unlike Domino's, on that day we don't get a freebie if the deliverer tarries beyond a half-hour.

That day—ever so faithful to the Apostle, Luther called it the "stundenlein," the "occasio," "the hour," "that day." The decisive moment—it's there in our sacrament—the hour cometh and now is . . .

It is there in our recessional, the Southern folk hymn:

> What "wondrous love" is this, O my soul
> What wondrous love is this that caused
> the Lord of bliss to bear the "dreadful curse"
> for my soul.

It is there in Kathy Heetland's lovely rendition of Vaughan Williams's plaintive "Rosamunde Prelude" and "The Wondrous Love" postlude. In this sacred season of light and darkness, of warmth and cold, of hope and fear, we ponder the eschatological break-in of God's judgment and mercy. The Trinity sings the song. Deus Absconditus and Deus Adventus explains the enigma of history full of hope and impending doom. He who has come and is coming illumines the strange paradox of our human condition, glorious and tragic. The restless spirit of God, consoling yet uncanny, makes us aware of the at once infinite distance yet sublime nearness of time and eternity. God, son and spirit exude that day—wondrous love.

In biblical purview, "that day" is expressed in many ways: the Day of the Lord, Day of Judgment, Day of the Messiah, Day of Christ, Day of God, Day of visitation, Coming Day. In the history of theology, liturgy and music, it becomes *Dies Irae*: the day of wrath. "Wondrous Love" has an equally rich derivation and tradition often a counterpoint or transformer point to "that day." The wondrous works of the Psalms become the wondrous feat of deliverance and covenant. The wondrous loving-kindness of the shepherd of Israel becomes the wondrous love of Jesus.

That day can be understood in at least four ways:

1. It can be Yaweh's justice in the crises of nations and history.

2. It can be Christ's sublime parousia—the second coming.

3. It can be the day of our own reckoning or dying.

4. It can be today—now.

## Second Sermons

### 1.

Trace these four senses of "that day." In a primal sense "that day" is when Yaweh joins human events in battle. Gerhard von Rad and Robert Jewett have shown that the zeal of the Lord performs in history the justice that alone grounds peaceable kingdom. In some mysterious, that is, holy way, historic crisis is always "that day of the Lord." The last rocket launch in Bosnia, a fateful meeting of Israel and Syria, can be "that day." We recall the powerful *Dies Irae* tapestry in Coventry Cathedral, England, built onto the bombed skeleton of that church destroyed on those nights of November 14 and 15, 1940. "That day" cries from the ruins of Kaiser Wilhelm memorial church in Berlin and from the rubble of mosques in Sarajevo, the slaughter warehouse in Srebrenica, and the bloodstained floor of the Cathedral in Rwanda.

"That day" is Cyrus the Persian or Nebuchadnezzer the Babylonian. It is the Syro/Ephraimite Alliance, the German/Japanese concordat, the Sino/Soviet Pact. It is the day when nations conspire against the Lord.

History and supervening, *Heilsgeschichte* is "that day."

### 2.

"That day" is also the day of Christ—the hour of Christ's awaited appearance. Christ's consummation of history and nature will happen in time and space as he returns to judge the living and the dead. The kingdom for which we keep watch is also a coming that transcends those orders. As Ray Brown has shown in *The Birth of the Messiah,* there is a haunting historical quality to Advent and Second Advent. Standing at the close of two millennia of delayed parousia, we can only sigh with W.B. Yeats'"Twenty centuries of stony sleep vexed to nightmare by a rocking cradle . . ." Yet how silently, how silently the wondrous gift is given—Maranatha, come, Lord Jesus . . . My Kingdom is within you.

### 3.

Again, "that day" may be our day of reckoning, of awakening, of epiphany. It may be that ordinary bush—burning, yet not consumed. It may be some call . . . "man, woman, where are you?" It may be the vocation of some still small voice. Some calls may reverberate against our frail, finite mortal existence. Dying day comes to each of us and to all whom we love. "That day" came three weeks ago to the home across from ours, when Claire and Bernie burned to death in a motel fire in Kentucky, leaving three young boys. Even if we are spared some premature death by violence, even if we are granted Dr. King's dream of long years, that day inevitably comes . . . When hearts fail or we cannot breathe or malignancy or senility still body or mind. When infectious heat overwhelms us and the "fever of life is over, our work is then done." "The day of dread," said Luther, "is God's gift to us, awakening within us the need for forgiveness." That day brings all into perspective and priority. I have built my house and filled my barns, said one, "take your ease" (Luke 12:18 ff). "Fool, this night, that day your soul is required of you." Therefore, in the ultimate sense, that day is always this day. "Today . . . if you will hear my voice."

4.

Today is the implosion of yesterday and tomorrow in God's time. Today is that day. Today is the juncture of heretofore and everafter. Wondrous love is therefore the imperishable bread amid the blaze and substance of "that day." Love is the radiant, high energy dot at the center of that collapsing black hole amid the expanding 40 billion galaxies.

Justice is mercy, mercy is justice. Without mercy, justice is petulance; without justice, mercy is cheap debilitating indulgence. At the axis point of history, at the crux of it all, justice has been transfigured into grace. It happened on a wondrous cross on which a prince of glory ignominiously died. Wrath has been transformed into wondrous love.

In his enigmatic, though rhapsodic *Ethics*, Dietrich Bonhoeffer wrote of this reconciliation:

> In the figure of the reconciler is revealed the secret of God.
> The abyss of God's love encompasses even the most abysmal
> godlessness of the world. In a manner which passes all comprehension,
> God reverses the judgment of justice and piety, declares himself guilty
> toward the world and thereby wipes out the world's guilt.[2]

---

2. Bonhoeffer, *Ethics*, 9.

It is as if in kenotic emptying God's wrath diminishes back on the Omega point of sheer love.

So we are left with that wondrous day of love. One of the most moving scenes of this assimilation is in Giordano's opera, *Andrea Chenier*. The aria "La Mama Morta" becomes the epiphany scene in the film *Philadelphia*. Maddalena returns home during the French Revolution to find her house incinerated and her dead mother at the door. She wails:

> They killed my mother at the door of my room;
> She died. she saved me. I looked; the place that cradled me was burning.

In words of George Bernano's, "The prisoner of his agony" becomes the possessor of Christ's wondrous love. In the film *Philadelphia*, the young attorney played by Tom Hanks is fired from the firm even as he is dying from AIDS. Like Maddalena, though all around is destroyed, he finds sustenance for that impending day in such wondrous love. "Do you pray?" he asks his lawyer, played by Denzel Washington. And as he is transported by Maddalena's song in that hour, that night, that day, both discover amid oblivion, amid abyss in the grim face of death—love. The bread come down from heaven, the bread of immeasurable, wondrous, unqualified love. As the young priest receives last rites, a dying benediction is uttered in Bernanos' *Diary of a Country Priest*, he faintly whispers, "toute la grace: all is grace."

From the verge of oblivion, the abyss, within Dali's descending arc of the universe we sit at cosmic supper—an eternal feast.

One of the windows of this chapel celebrates the appearance here in 1954 at the World Council of Churches Assembly of the missionary statesman D. T. Niles. He once defined Evangelism as "one beggar telling another beggar where to find bread."

Our scriptures Isaiah 58 and Matthew 5 and 25 tell the same story. Rightful fast before God is the feast of human sustenance just as salt is the salience and leaven of life. The leaven of justice is the bread of mercy. The antidote of sin is the tincture of compassion. Worship and prayer without justice is noise however solemn. Our proper response to the day of wrath is to do justice and love mercy. Beggar to beggar, we are to lead one another to the hearth of wrath, become the hearth of mercy. There we find sustaining bread and the refreshing cup. To reenact the Isaianic and Messianic vocation is to feed the hungry as we are being fed, heal the sick as we are being made whole and bring good news to the poor as, impoverished, we are being made rich.

The sacrament before us now is the mystery of that day become wondrous love. We realize with the General in *Babette's Feast* that mercy is infinite. Here at altar mercy and truth are met together as righteousness and bliss kiss. The love feast before us is the conjunction of God's justice and mercy. The commensal meal is both Christ's searching exposé and his saving rendezvous. "That day" and "wondrous love" here co-mingle. They cohere in our sure redeemer, whom we now greet.[3]

---

3. Comment: This sermon continues to capture my imagination. As I write today in the first week of Advent 2014, the juxtaposition of seemingly contradictory themes—love and judgement seems almost as the essence of the faith. As Rilke has said in *Rilke's Book of Hours*:

> I love the dark hours of my being.
> My mind deepens into them.
> There I can find, as in old letters,
> the days of my life, already lived,
> and held like a legend, and understood.
> Then the knowing comes: I can open
> to another life that's wide and timeless.
> So I am sometimes like a tree
> rustling over a gravesite
> and making real the dream
> of the one its living roots
> embrace: a dream once lost
> among sorrows and songs.

# 16

# Righteousness[1]

"Walk the talk," goes the saying, and so says our text.

Proclamation and performance ought to coincide.

In this vein our lectionary passage extols the inseparability of Gospel plus law, grace and works.

This obvious certainty of the moral connection of word and act makes Jesus opening words of this harsh denunciation—as Matthew remembered it—most startling.

The Rabbis, scribes and pharisees, sit in Moses' seat.

What they teach, observe and follow—don't be put off by what they do . . . reject their duplicity, have no part of their hypocrisy.

"Do as they *say* not as they do."

These words resonate with those addressed to the false ministers by Paul in Romans.

You teach not to commit adultery and you commit adultery.

You preach not to steal and you steal.

When you judge, you judge yourself because you do the very thing you condemn.

Paul is here condemning the audacity of every self-righteous put down—the illusion of judgementless judgment . . . weak of strong, Jew of gentile, man of woman, slave of free, rich of poor.

Together and in synergy faith and works constitute authentic piety.

1. Sermon first delivered at Garrett Seminary. Matt 23:1–12.

## RIGHTEOUSNESS

Faith mutates the deceptive self satisfaction of works. Works sublimate the smug ecstacy of faith.

In the theme of this Reformation festival, faith and works belong together in the order of salvation. They are integral. You can't have one without the other.

Professor Dick Tholin of Garrett reminded us of this conjunction in his convocation when he asked: "Who is my neighbor?"

What must I do to obtain eternal life? Answer—

One journeyed from Jerusalem to Jericho and fell among thieves.

Which passerby was the neighbor?

Eternal life?—the binding of wounds?—sounds like Jesus' inaugural.

The blind see, the lame walk . . .

But on deeper reflection if we dissect the dynamics of *hamartia* and *soteria*—sin and saving—we find a total synthesis of faith and works. Righteousness is this composite belief and behavior.

Faithful works have radiated out of the Garrett watchtower this fall. Stacey and Leigh, and Sunjay and Justine (Cherokee child of my student nearly decapitated in auto accident)—and each of you on whose watch faith has prompted acts of mercy (students and their children who sustained profound injuries).

Faith and works . . .

Now I'm aware that such an association may not appear obvious, especially to this crazy culture that thinks health care means lawsuits, public housing means demolition, muscle-flexing means peacemaking, and to reform means to dismantle—suddenly evil means good.

The joint declaration is being signed this week in Lutherstadt. Augsburg explores this synthesis of faith and works.

Lutherans and Protestants generally tend to accent faith over works.

Catholics, like Jews and Muslims, emphasize the moral life.

Now the joint declaration on justification by faith says, in so many words, "we both had it wrong in exaggerating unilaterally either faith or works."

Decrying the disjunction, the declaration cries out for conjunction— "get it back together."

In its stirring words: "The justified live by faith that comes from the Word of Christ and is active through love the fruit of the spirit. Participating in Christ's body and blood—they live righteously in accord with the will of God."

We need to rejoin those disjoined loose ends which always threaten to tear apart soul and society.

After all Jesus, James and John spoke of the danger:

If you love me keep my commandments . . .

Faith without works is dead . . . Loving God and not the neighbor is a lie . . .

When we split this synergy, symbolic existence becomes diabolic. When that sewn together is torn apart, when integrity becomes insularity—life goes bad.

We're left with what Simone Weil calls *Gerissenheit*—"torn-apartness."

The grand biblical synthesis is clear: Justification by grace to faith for works.

"We are His workmanship," writes Paul to Ephesus, "created in Christ Jesus for good works."

Faithful works or working faith was what the world was made for. The gift was for the task, claimed Luther—*Gabe/Aufgabe*.

Commenting on Calvin's careful crafting of the faith and works issue, Paul Lehmann writes: "the praxis of the Gospel as law is the nurture of the obedience of faith . . . Luther," continues Lehmannn, "taught that the decalogue provided the church and world the true and lively way of the practice of the Gospel as law."

For the traditions of Israel, the seat of Moses, which is the final authority for Jesus, the purposes of humanity is Tikkun Olam—to heal the earth. Because of the fracture that we brought to the world, to be healed with God in order to bring healing in the earth required that the breach be bridged, the rift overcome, the dungeon be broken open.

Messias-Christus had to come all the way out here from eternity. He had to go all the way down to death and hell—had to accept the Akedic ropes—the burden of *pecatta mundi*—the sin of the world.

*Christ lag in Todesbanden*—tied down by the bands of humanity's sin and death we are 'righteoused' by this faithfulness.

> Being purified by this sacrifice
> envisioned and awakened by that quickening ray
> we are raised from the tower and placed on the watchtower.
> The redeemed sinner becomes God's citadel in the world.

This is the meaning of the Reformation.

Some of us are now reading Karl Barth's *Romerbrief* (our campus book of the year)—the book which sounded the alarm of grace as the megaevil of human pretension (WWI) and threatened to destroy the earth at the dawn of this century.

Considered by many to be the most important religious title of this century, Garrett's own William Hordern called Barth the herald of the "new reformation." Commenting on "Christ the power of God unto salvation" in Romans 1:16, he offers these words:

"In this world we find ourselves imprisoned . . . Our desertion of the One who gives us life is complete. Yet the Gospel announces the transformation of our creaturliness into freedom. It proclaims the forgiveness of sins, the restitution of the ability to live rightly in Him, the victory over death."

From being brought low in the tower of degradation we have been set on high in the watchtower. "He made me a watchman upon the city wall." We are saved to serve.

Barth continues:

> Bound to the world as it is we cannot here and now apprehend . . . we can only receive the Gospel for it is the recollection of God which is created by the Gospel that comprehends in its meaning the whole burden of sin, the whole curse of death, which still oppresses us, still locks us down . . .

This recollection is the commemorative table around which we gather today. . .

Barth continues:

"The resurrection is both barrier and exit for this barrier becomes the frontier of a new country."

We have therefore in the power of God a lookout—a door—a hope.

We take, in Luther's words a simple little step in despair which is its own consolation.

Luther says that Grace makes the law, that constriction that was death, now dear to us. The law is no longer against us but with us. It is a way out.

The prisoner, concludes Barth, becomes a watchman.

In Charles Wesley's moving poetry:

> Long my imprisoned spirit lay, fastbound in sin and nature's night—
> Thine eye diffused a quickening ray, I woke, the dungeon flamed with light . . . My chains fell off, my heart was free, I rose, went forth, and followed thee.
> And those redeemed itinerants followed into fields and slums, prisons and markets—working out that salvation.

That reformation release has changed lives and changed history. As Luther lies bound in belly and conscience in the Augustinian tower . . . and German troops in binding service sack Rome, causing Machiavelli to lament the end of the Renaissance . . .

Erasmus, another true reformer and true catholic, affirms the freedom of the will, like Luther puts the New Testament into the language of the people, and builds a watchtower of liberty for ages to come.

At about the same time King Henry VIII, that wayward son, heraldedas defender of the faith for his wrongheaded refutation of Luther's sacramental theology, having bound seemingly countless wives into London Tower, begins to ponder Luther and build a Tudor watchtower, which will ground a prayerbook and a piety that will transform world history through Anglican, Puritan, and Wesleyan revolutions.

Meanwhile, in 1527, Luther sinks into the bondage of deep depression and so sees in those pre-Prozac days, the strength of God alone against the duel of sabre-rattling *Anfechtung*, composing *Ein Feste Burg*, which our Roman Catholic neighbors now sing lustily. In his boorish way, a bull in the vineyard manages to plant a garden fashioned in freedom, democracy and an upsurge of grace and liberation. That strong tower, built up from the cross of Christ, still towers o'er the wrecks of time, watching over the violence and the victory released by the Reformation, even into our own turbulent history.

Shall we mention that other Martin Luther in the Birmingham jail?

Or Mandela in his costal dungeon in South Africa? Or Solzhenitsyn in the Gulag? Or Aung San Suu Kyi under house arrest in Burma?

From the burden of bondage has been fashioned the freedom of faith.

The tower has become the watchtower.

As on that night when that unsurpassable one was dropped into Caiaphas' dungeon just beyond Jerusalem's south wall.

After supping for the last before forever in that Essene manner above that ominous Kedron valley . . . adjourning to that garden with those gnarled olive trees, not for a sherry, but for sweat and tears . . .

> The cost of failed righteousness . . .
> and on the horizon that hill and that burial cave
> . . . to redeem, that is prison break, us all in that glorious dawn escape
> So come now and sup with Him, for all is ready.[2]

---

2. Comments: I loved the opportunity provided by the seminary to be both teacher and preacher, pastoral confidant to students and officient at the sacrament. The kind of

# 17

# Reconciliation[1]

THANK YOU FOR THE privilege of speaking with you this morning from this pulpit distinguished this last quarter century by my dear friend David Irwin. Our friendship goes back thirty years to when we were young theologians terrorizing together the haunts of Edinburgh. Fortunately for the peace of the city and ourselves we both met our "bonnie lassies" and in the words of the old hymn—"our travelling days were done!"

Neither of us would have thought in 1961 that the span of our ministries would be marked by such momentous events. For him, it was the bitter saga of the Ireland story. For me, it was the U.S. history of the Civil Rights movement and the Viet Nam and subsequent wars. Throughout these trying years, we were upheld by peoples like yourselves—partner communities on the journey of faith as we sought to discern the "signs of the times" seeking all the while to see if there was any "Word from the Lord."

The Word from the Lord often comes in Isaianic comfort: "Your warfare is over and your iniquity is pardoned" (Isa 40). Perhaps this word

---

mutually supportive community was a deep joy in the concluding years of my working career.

1. This sermon was initially preached in Groomsport Presbyterian Church, Northern Ireland, June 2, 1997. Texts: Genesis 4:3–16; 1 John 1:5–9. The message, entitled then: "Primal Crime/Ultimal Peace," sought to address the enigmas of ready revenge and elusive reconciliation in the recent history of Ireland. It then anchored these eternal truths of transcendental violence and discovered peace in other events of world history and in the history of the Bible.

eventually comes in despicable and weary human war like Ireland or Jewish and Muslim strife in the Middle East.

This morning, as we meet here in war-weary Ireland we receive such a refreshing and forgiving word. Scripture speaks of an unending cycle of human violence derivative of the fratricidal strife symbolized by the Cain-Abel story. Yes there was a violent crime of disobedience, exile, and murder in Eden and east of Eden. This primal crime also triggers a process of redemption in world history as the earth groans in hope for its deliverance, the furtherance and sustenance of creation (Rom 8). The ultimal peace is never fully realized in our own human time and place, but it is surely secured in the new city of God where there will be "no more tears" (Rev 22). For now, we can only confess in shame and repentence—in Ireland and Israel—with the stern rebuke of Rabbi Michael Lerner of Tikkun, " the way of Judaism has been murdered by the State of Israel" (or the states of Ireland).

## DATELINE BAGHDAD

Today (2004), chaos reigns in Afghanistan, Lybia, Iraq, and Syria. In 1991 The Kurds had struck a deal with the Sadaam Hussein government to begin forming their own homeland of Kurdistan. Many peoples still wander the earth homeless: Palestine, Armenia, Israel, Tibet, Salvador. Could it be that the great rendezvous of East and West—hinted in Scripture is about to appear—beginning in Mesopotamia? Where did this conflict begin—where will it end?

    Iraq's attack on Kuwait
        America's ill-conceived support for the Shah
            Israel's illegal occupation of the West Bank and Palestine
    The Nazi holocaust which made the implantation of Israel necessary
        The British mistakes in Mesopotamia
            The expulsion of the Jews from Europe in early modernity
            The medieval pogroms
    The failure of Babylonian Judaism and Jewish Christianity
        The Roman destruction of the Temple and the Nation of Israel
            On and on back to Cain and the primal crime of Eden and E. Eden

Reconciliation

## DATELINE JERUSALEM

It is October 8 of 1996. The pious *Hasidim*—old men in black hats and clothes sway back and forth at the Wailing Wall—the only remaining façade of Herod's Temple. Above on the top of the mount is Al Asque Mosque—built on the spot where Mohammad took his leap of faith into heaven. Close at hand was Golgotha and the adjacent spots where Jesus was crucified, died, and ascended. Up top, restless and agitated Palestinian youth gathered on the mount. A counter-demonstration of Jewish extremists gathered and formed a parade. As the crowd grew, angry boys pelted the police below with stones. As police will, they fired live ammo at the David sling-shot wannabees, and as dusk settled nineteen Palestinians were dead, with more to follow. Where will it end? Where did it begin?

 The massacre Sharon ordered on the Palestinian refugee camps
  The 1967 war
  The Warsaw Ghetto
   The Christian crusaders exterminating the Jews of Munich
   The Bar Kochba revolt in 150
    Cyrus and the Babylonia captivity
 The Hebrew exodus from Egypt and the cleansing of the Caananites
 And on and on we go—back to the primal crime of Cain.

## DATELINE BELFAST

We Americans come home to Ireland. We don't visit or sightsee. We come home. To the hills of County Down—or the setting sun on Galway Bay—we're going home. No land has so deeply shaped the American character as this Emerald Isle. The Scots-Irish immigrations of the eighteenth century and the migrations during the potato famine of the nineteenth have made us the people we are.

As we drove up this week through the Republic and into Northern Ireland, we became aware again of our precious and precarious heritage. Then one passes through the tanks and barricades and the border villages where so many have been killed, or into West Belfast and Shankhill wall. And arriving during these days of promise when Peter Brooke tries to set the table at Storemont for Unionist and Nationalist to "come and reason together," we become aware again of the flight of the dove and descent of the serpent—the downward coil of evil and the upward spiral of hope.

## Second Sermons

Where will it end? Where did it begin?

  Was it the Gibralter 3
    The Shankhill Butchers or the Birmingham 6
      The Darclay massacre or Bloody Sunday in Londonderry
        The partition or the solemn league
          The Battle of the Bogne in 1690
      The plantation of the Scots by King James or the killing of the natives
        Those future British campaigns against Ireland by King Richard II
          The Scots incursions from Ireland against the Roman Britons
      The violent Indoeuropean migrations against the Atlantic peoples
        Fin MacCool and the giant causeway to Scotland
          The two swimming brothers and the right hand
            Cain and Abel

And so on and on and we are back to the primal crime of Cain. We could speak of India or South Africa. The tale is always the same. We find ourselves like Shakespeare's *Richard III*, "So deep in blood that sin plucketh sin" (Act 4, Line 64, 65).

The tale would be sad and tragic were not that primal and perpetual crime countered in the history of God by the primal and perpetual love of God—the descent into hell and the ascent into glory of Jesus, the Christ.

Political events are also pregnant or portentous in another way.

In his great historical novel *Les Miserables*, Victor Hugo expresses the idea that historical events though seeming to be purposeless as if subject only to chance and vicissitude are actually directed by a higher power, what the Bible calls judgment. Reflecting on the Battle of Waterloo and the defeat of Napoleon, Hugo writes that the apparent and immediate cause was the failure of reinforcements to arrive because some peasants gave them a bum steer. I quote: "because on the afternoon of a certain summer's day, a shepherd said to a Prussian in the forest, 'go this way and not that.' But the real cause was more profound." Hugo writes:

> End of the dictatorship. A whole European system crumbled away. Was it possible that Napoleon should have won the battle? We answer no—why? Because of Wellington? Because of Blucher? No—Because of God . . . Napoleon had been denounced in the infinite and his fall had been decided on. He embarrassed God. Waterloo is not a battle; it is a change of front on part of the universe.[2]

2. Hugo, *Les Miserables*, bk. 1, ch. 19.

## Reconciliation

To see what is really going on behind the scenes, we must not only look with the eyes of faith but act as if peace had already overwhelmed crime. In love Christ has overcome crime. "He has broken down the dividing wall of hostility" (Eph 2:14). That human construction may be in Jerusalem, Berlin or on Shankhill road. But it has already been undermined by the upheaval of God.[3]

Our President, Jimmy Carter, was a wall-breaker. He could put his arms on the shoulders of leaders Begin and Sadat and say, "Gentlemen—let us pray." Obviously he was run out of office. The world cannot abide such "redeemers" without fierce resistance.

God in Christ is present in the world. He stands beside us silently as he stood beside the Grand Inquisitor in Seville. He seeks to reverse the downward swirling calamity into an upward swirling spring of love.

Psalm 90 gathers this humiliation and exaultation into one grand picture:

> Lord, You have been our dwelling place in all generations
> Before the mountains were brought forth or ever Thou hads't formed the earth and the world,
> Even from everlasting to everlasting Thou art God.
> Thou turnest man to destruction and sayest, return ye children of men
> For a thousand years in the sight are but as yesterday, when it is past
> And a watch in the night . . .
> Thou hast set our iniquities before thee, our secret sins in the light of thy countenance . . .
> For all our days are passed away in thy wrath, We spend our years as a tale that is told
> So teach us to number our days that we may apply our hearts unto wisdom.

St. Augustine, in *The City of God*, showed us how we were all engulfed in that primal and perpetual crime. He called it original sin. He was not speaking genetics but genesis. The empirical fact is that we look around we see an intricate web of fault and guilt which we have woven—carrying us all into a bondage from which we yearn for redemption. The fibers of this history entangle our history to this day.

---

3. Think of Robert Frost: "Something there is that doesn't love a wall." In Frost, *In the Clearing*.

Pause for a moment to consider the momentous seventeenth century in British and world history. The English Revolution, from which the myriad revolutions of world history would evolve, American, French, Russian, was taking place. Charles I had lost his head, and the Westminster Assemblies of the Puritans produced the documents of freedom and civility that would reconstitute the orders of the world.

Cromwell's revolt was castigated and America was derisively called the "Presbyterian Revolt." About the time of Cromwell's campaign in Ireland, Thomas Hobbes wrote about the state and the state of nature using the highly charged biblical word—Leviathan—the whale.

"I have spoken," he writes, "of the natural kingdom of God and his natural laws." I add this short declaration on his natural punishments:

"There is no action of man in this life, that is not the beginning of so long a chain of consequences, as no human providence is high enough to give man a prospect to the end. Intemperance is naturally punished with diseases, negligent government with rebellion—rebellion with slaughter." (*Leviathan*)

Hobbes is brutally honest about the "Wages of Sin." The Bible is even more candid about the consequences of our actions: the fall and all of its terror—its never-ending cycle of retribution—what the Greeks called Nemesis. The Bible claims that we have been lifted from the bottomless quicksand pit—the mire from which we can't escape. On Holy Saturday, Christ descended into the deep recesses of the serpent—gathering all captivity into himself—and delivering us back to God. The Bible answers the volcano of evil with the descent and ascent of the dove of reconciliation.

In this summer season of the church year, we celebrate Ascension and Pentecost. Whitsunday in Ireland is marked with roses and peonies, chlamidia and pansies; all symbolize the victory of life over death, beauty over disgrace, color and light over darkness, growth over degradation. Christ ascended reigns over the world. Hobbes' natural sanctions and tragic necessity no longer hold sway. The grinding treadmill has been stopped. Grace has overwhelmed sin, law, and determinism. Now grace opens up the new world of freedom, opportunity, and reconciliation. Where first Adam fell down, this New Adam—humanity in Christ, rises up in victory. Primal crime has yielded to ultimate peace.

How do we see and bring about this new world? In mystical and moral vision, we now see life and world as it ought, and should have been, and in the deep recesses of God and the creation it really was. We are given new eyes to see. The mystic now sees the hidden in ordinary experiences.

It was just another burning bush in the desert—or was it?

He was just another Passover traveler on the road to Emmaus—or was he?

It was just another one sick and imprisoned, hungry, sick or homeless—or was it?—When did we see You . . . ?

In the Name of the Father, Son, and Spirit—Amen.[4]

---

4. Comments: This sermon highlights a penchant of mine—to look at historical events in terms of polarities—even blacks and whites configured as "good guys and bad guys." I know this way of thinking and writing simplifies the complexities of real life. The Bible also comes close to such Manichean designations at certain times and places. When historical and political events are saturated with religious fervor we often cast them in this dualistic light. The older I get the more I seek the wisdom of Walt Kelly and the Pogo quip: "We have met the enemy and he is us."

# 18

# True Man[1]

OUR LECTIONARY TEXTS CATCH us by surprise as the weariness of the holiday wears on and we can't really get up for any more. First there's SHOPPING—up Michigan Ave. at Bloomingdales—where I've been teaching Bible this year at 4th Church—lots of toys—gold toothpicks, a stuffed camel, a new cell phone or tablet—now we'll have to find someone to call or text. Then there's SOMEONE COMING—A homecoming of sorts—that crazy uncle Jack comes back for Christmas dinner and the ham and dressings and resentments start flying—or maybe it's SPORTS—and the Bulls and Bears are already out of it. Only the Blackhawks are still there—guess we better get ready for Cubs' baseball—RIGHT!

This boredom and sadness and disappointment is now shattered by two readings. As worldwide lectionary, they are heard round the world—this Sunday and next—they go right to the center of the mystery that this faux celebration of ours should really be about and find its authentic heartland: Matthew 2 and John 1. The church and world have mulled them over now for 2000 years, and we still only have a faint glimmer of what they mean—the deepest truths ever heard on this earth—what is TRUE HUMAN and TRUE GOD?

---

1. As another year was about to roll over—I offered this duet of sermons at Second Presbyterian Church, Chicago. "Excursus: True Human, True God. In the written text I use the long dash repeatedly to show the staccato rhythm of the delivered message. December 29, 2013 Text: Matthew 2. Second Pres., Chicago.

## True Man

TRUE HUMAN (authentic anthropology) is the first thing that Scripture and tradition want to teach us. Our text is about a very down-to-earth family, a baby, a young son going out as a teacher, a Rabbi. Following birth in a cow's straw basket— in a no-place of the world—he is a refugee in Egypt. The authorities are hunting him down, He has nowhere to lay his head down and rest. Yes, the Kings or Magi are impressive—they carry three luxury items scarcely found—even in Bloomingdales: gold, frankincense, myrrh—exotic substances from exotic places—but they come and in a moment are gone.

Christianity pushes its way into this world between two exaggerating faiths—Gnosticism and Marcionism on the one hand, excessively otherworldly—and Judaism and Islam on the other—excessively worldly. Now don't worry if that sentence sails off into space—explication would involve the whole course on the history of religion. Leave it at this: the Gnostic and Marcionite movements almost won the day from the infant church. The gnostics mistakingly believed that they alone were saved by special knowledge, and the followers of Marcion believed that the Hebrew Bible was evil and had to be cut away. The movements were and still are too spiritual for Jesus, God, and Scripture.

As for Jews and proto-Muslims—at about Jesus' time they had good and true insights into God's kingdom but they each thought that Jesus was not God, and could not be God if he suffered and died—so they kept him as a teacher and prophet, a great man, but nothing more, certainly not the redeemer, savior and Lord of the world. Such views still threaten to throw us off track in this created and incarnated world. Leave it for now that this—our Christmas child—even as he becomes the Good Friday and Easter child—is one who came to and for this earth. He is TRUE HUMAN.

The songs all sing it:

> With the poor and mean and lowly, lived on earth, our savior holy, day by day like us he grew
> Tears and smiles like us he knew, he feels our sadness and shares our gladness
> The scriptures spell it out:
> He was like us in all things—He knew our infirmities—He was tempted in every way like us—yet without sin (Heb 4:15)
> Jesus is the power of God for salvation . . . first to the Jew then to the Greek [Romans 1:16]
> Made a little lower than the angels—that he should taste death for all men (Heb 2:9)

> He was made low like all of us so that he could reconcile the sins of all people (Heb 2:17)
> He offered up crying and tears—He learned obedience by the things he suffered (Heb 5:8)
> God has chosen the poor and simple of the world to bring down the rich and wise [James +Corinthians]

Why do the apostles, evangelists, early church leaders and theologians across the centuries make so much of Jesus' humanity? Why must he be received and believed to be the TRUE HUMAN? Here is the argument: First—a supernatural, divine being cannot empathize and sympathize with us down into the very fiber, heart, mind, conscience and soul of our human being. There is no way such a pure divinity can know our human condition and need. King James had to become a commoner to talk to his people.

Secondly, Jesus is the only true and complete human being who ever lived. All human beings fall short not only of being like God but of being truly human. We fall short in body and mind—in justice and love, in aloneness and community. Thomas Aquinas—probably Christendom's only theologian who knew Judaism and Islam thoroughly through his study of Avicenna and Maimonides—taught that Jesus as perfect man and perfect God—enabled us to be fully human.

True God alone couldn't do it. Neither could true human alone. True God/Man was needed.

John Calvin, who best brought this Thomistic Christian heritage to us in the Reformed and Presbyterian movement, said that our fulfilled humanity is the first desire of God in our creation. In teaching which has given rise in history to fully secular life: economics, arts, politics, public education, culture, environment, society, family, we are taught not to escape and be rid of this world but to care, tend, and steward it to its full creative potential.

This Matthew material is in good part why the newborn church in a few short centuries confessed these two messages in the Apostles' and Nicene Creeds: He was born to Mary under Herod, suffered under Pilate—was crucified, dead and buried and then he rose . . . a fully human and historical identity and—and it's a big and weighty assertion: Yes, he was Very God of Very God, begotten not made, not confined or constricted by his humanity, rather fully released to his humanity by his divinity as he is fully given his divinity by his humanity—but let's save that for next week. For now we dwell on the fact that he is TRUE PERSON, TRUE MAN,

# True Man

TRUE WOMAN, TRUE CHILD, TRUE YOUTH, TRUE ELDER, TRUE HUMAN.

The text it seems to me is a text about finding our human selves and our bearings in the birth of the messiah. (I here use Raymond Brown on his classic book: *The Birth of the Messiah* (Doubleday, 1993) First, we are world—people and people of the world.

The text has three couplets: The Magi come to Jerusalem, Herod asks the scribes—"where is he who is born?" Herod asks Magi to find the child and return to him. Then we have three matching verses: Magi go to Jerusalem, Magi find the child and offer gifts and the Magi depart and do not return to Herod. We have here a life and death journey of three kings—symbols of the search of all humanity for the One—both God and human.

The Magi were Zoroastrian priests—astrologers—who plotted earth bearings on this planet which we thought was an endless plate—from planets in the sky—Saturn, Jupiter, and the others, They were from Anatolia—translated—the East. One black guy was from Somalia (frankincense). The Gospel originates in the Orient and proceeds toward the Occident. It is headed for the Middle and ultimately out to the Western world—gentile lands—We're talking about Arabia, Africa, Somalia, Egypt, and finally Jerusalem and Bethlehem, then out to Greece, Rome, Europe, the Americas. We live on one inhabited earth: Jerusalem, Rome, Chicago, Bejing and back home, and He's "got the whole world" and the little bitsy baby in his hand.

## THREE KINGS FOLLOWED, WHILE ONE SNARLED[2]

The winter days become long and dark. Christmastide now ends with these strange twelve days concluding not with "twelve drummers drumming" but with a bright heavenly flash called Epiphany. Now I suppose we ought to be perfectly politically correct and call these "happy holidays." In any case, we now begin our secular "Holy Year," which begins with a New Year's hangover and ends with another Elvis or Johnny Cash "Blue Christmas." Even in the liturgical year these days, we find ourselves in darkness shrouding piercing light. Three great Scandinavian films capture the dreary yet dreamy mood of the season. Of course we begin with *Babette's Feast*. Bergman's *Winter Light* catches the despair of existence, as its pastor can find no

---

2. Here are my additional notes on the three kings, which was research for a sermon in Riverside, Illinois. Sermon preached at Riverside Presbyterian Church, New Years Day, 2006.

reason to dissuade his parishioner from suicide. Sara's and my favorite, with which we often celebrate the end of courses with our students, is *Italian for Beginners*. Here even the deranged Pastor Wedermeyer's mad rantings after he has been removed by the Bishop cannot quench the flame of a happier new ministry—perhaps a parable of RPC. Some of you also ask us about reading for the season. We recommend Jimmy Carter's *Our Endangered Values* and Hosseni's *Kite Runner*.

The lectionary Gospel reading for Epiphany offers a similar admixture of light and darkness.

"Now when Jesus was born in Bethlehem of Judea in the days of Herod the King, behold there came wise men from the East to Jerusalem [in Greek—*majon apo Anatolon*/shamin priests from Anatolia]. They asked 'where is he, who is born King of the Jews for we have seen his star in the East and have come to worship him.' When Herod the King had heard these things he was troubled—and all Jerusalem with him" (Matt 2:1–3).

## THE COMMUNION MEDITATION: THREE KINGS FOLLOWED/ANOTHER TREMBLED

Why the hope on the one part? Why the rage on the other? Herein lies the secret of the gospel. Consider the hope, the fear, and the resolution.

Hope arises in this natal star because it arises over and attracts the whole world. "Rise, shine, your light is come and the Glory of the Lord is risen upon thee."

Consider the following points:

A star or comet was said to signal and herald the birth of Alexander the Great, Caesar, and Cyrus the King of Persia. Yet only this child-King of Bethlehem has really made a decisive difference. No person born since that birth can ever be the same again. Only this one came to redeem the world, and only he accomplished such deliverance.

He was the expected offspring of David—the King of the Jews and therefore the King of Kings. He was "the star that shone out of Jacob and the scepter that rose out of Israel." He was that light to whom all the world would come. In the words of Psalm 68, he was the one who led humanity on high. He was the captive who himself would lead captivity captive, the one to whom kings would come bearing their gifts.

This was Isaiah's little child—an *Enfant Mirable*—yet so much more. As we noted in Advent, this child would pave again the highway to God—he would restore Torah and righteousness. He would make the crooked straight, the rough places a plain, and the wilderness bloom. His name was wonderful, counselor (son of man), he was mighty God, everlasting Father (Son of God), Prince of Peace.

Epiphany signals light to the Gentiles—to the far coasts which await his law. The brightness of his coming is framed by Hanukkah's flame a century before and Bar Kochba's revolt (Israel's star child) a century later. Kindred radiance, reflective and corroborative illumination comes from Israel's star and Islam's crescent.

Who are these three kings? First, we're not talking about George Clooney and Ice Cube—though that was a great namesake film. In earliest tradition, these three represent the whole world. Casper is a white guy who can't jump—he brings the gift of gold—remember Adam Smith?—the wealth of nations. Melchior is black, from Africa—he bears frankincense—this resin was and still is the mainstay of the Somalia trade route, which runs through Mogadishu along the East African coast. Balthazar is an Asian man who brings myrrh—another tree sap which becomes a mortuary spice—an embalming perfume—which portends the dreaded destiny of this child. Marco Polo records that he visited the town of Saveh in Persia where all of the kings were to have originated—a child king come for all the world's children, a young king and an old king for all the adults and elders of the world.

The three kings may actually have been Jewish refugee sages or astrologers from back in Babylon, where a great exile Torah academy had arisen. Herodotus spoke of Zoroastrian priests from Persia—modern Iran and Armenia. If so, we can only pray that our political wise men today will not decide to repay the visit. If you are interested in pursuing further the identity of these traveling Magi, check out the scholar, wonderworker Simon Magus of Samaria in Acts ch. 8. Wherever we land on these great legends, let it be said that they represent the whole world, which is the realm of God's love and desire.

They represent Epiphany—light. We are not left in the dark. God's light—from creation—from Abraham on is "for the nations." "Your offspring shall be as the stars of the heavens." God's light has penetrated the darkness of this world: its disease and death, its injustice and unfairness, its war and oppression, its pain and discouragement, and that darkness can never put out that light regardless of how bleak things may now appear. For now, it is true, we live in *Finsternis*—in twilight—the twilight of the gods.

The joyous Christmas cantata of Bach is tinged with the sacred, wounded head—that little baby whose birthbed was with the animals, that youthful itinerant Rabbi with "nowhere to lay his head" is then cruelly crowned with thorns. Now this sacred head enlivens and enlightens his body, which is his church, which is this world, which as John Tavener knew is our *Sacramentum Mundi*.

Underneath and lurking around this blissful epiphany and visitation is Herod's infanticide. The love table of recognition around which we gather today is also the table of hate and rejection. "Which of you will betray me?" Will it be Herod, that pretender King of the Jews? He thought Rome had appointed him to secure the peace. He was a Jewish king. He represented realm and religion. Now subversion was underway. A usurper had arisen. Like Richard III or Henry VII, King Herod would not hesitate to kill any threat to his power—even his own children. We sang on Christmas Sunday of "Herod the King in his regime—all children young to slay." The Egyptian and Passover infanticides are reenacted in perpetuity. If you look closely, the star over the manger is a cross. Today a million children in Somalia and two million in Kenya are threatened with starvation and dehydration. So much for frankincense and myrrh. In Anatolia and Kashmir, thousands, made refugees by the earthquake, are dying of exposure in the cold hills. Children from forever to forever, often with their mothers, are exposed to cold, danger and death. Tonight in Chicago, there are 25,000 homeless on the streets—under the bridges and viaducts—in makeshift cardboard houses—hounded by our Herodian officials—who don't want anyone to see.

Chicago only has beds, shelter and food on a given night for 4,000 persons. Twenty-five persons have frozen on our streets this early winter—six in one week. I know—my students who work in the Night Ministry, which this church supports—bury them in the paupers' mass graves. The average age of those 25,000 homeless—nine years.

One verse of our sermon hymn captures the theme:

> Myrrh is mine a bitter perfume, breathes a life of gathering gloom
> Sorrowing, sighing, bleeding, dying, sealed in the stone-cold tomb.

When Pavarotti sang his Christmas concert in Montreal Cathedral, he always sang:

> *Agnus Dei qui tollis pecatta mundi—miserere nobis, dona nobis pacem*
> Lamb of God who takes up the sin of the world—have mercy on us.

## True Man

Grant us peace.

Herod's lethal search for the beloved child, the only begotten son who was given over that the world might be saved, is the paradigm for the story of salvation. In 1961, I rented a dear old working camel outside the south wall of Jerusalem, and we began the five mile ride to Bethlehem. In Ramah, just south of Jerusalem, I passed Rachel's tomb—she who wept for her children who are no more—Rachel would become the symbol for Israel's and humanity's inconsolable loss—the evangelist evokes this story to interpret Herod's infanticide.

Yet light shines, and Easter Messiah always follows Christmas Messiah.

He whose name shall be called wonderful becomes worthy as the lamb who was slain and hath redeemed us to God by his blood to receive power and riches, wisdom and strength, honor and glory and blessing (Rev 5:12).

The first 1000 years of the common era was a period of working out the Truth aspects of the messianic event of the Three Wise Men. A thirteenth-century text by that name is an interrogation—in Greek and Arabic—of the threesome, asking after their rational beliefs, their philosophical reasons, and their scientific principles. Our new professor of Interfaith Studies at Cambridge—Garth Fowden—finds here a synthesis of the three great paths to knowledge into a somewhat harmonious duet of Abraham and Aristotle.

Now in these recent holidays, we have seen from interstellar satellites and telescopes that we are looking into a vast cosmic whirlwind of planets, perhaps a billion of which are like earth—goldilocks planets they are called—not too hot or too cold—in which they would freeze or burn up—these spheres have water and therefore they likely could support the emergence as this planet has. In recent weeks, I have walked the streets where Stephen Hawking lives in Cambridge, England. He (if you know the new film, *The Theory of Everything*), is one who knows all about this magnificent cosmos which is ordered by time and space.

The plan of the cosmos is like the plan of salvation of which our text in Matthew speaks. The charting instruments here take us from the Jews to the Gentiles. That grounding and bearing is also about light. The Gospels are quoting Isaiah 60—"rise, shine, your light is come and the glory of the Lord will be revealed and all flesh shall see it together." The Messiah—the one who made the cosmic journey out to this tiny space—he was born and baptized, killed and raised. His life therefore is ministry to the yet unlocated and mislocated and that now becomes our ministry—we are God's eyes, ears and voices—hands, feet and hearts. He went home so we could take over—still in the eternal radiance of his light.

What does this mean for us—now? For one thing if we wish to be our human self—or if we want to find ourself as "a man or woman for others"—we find it here. Much theology focuses on the point—made most sharply by Dietrich Bonhoeffer—that Jesus is the "Man for others." The altruistic self is a gift of God given in that man. Here I believe that our Christmas Lord is Word and Logos, Messiah and Lord, Prophet and Mahdi. He may even be Buddha and Krishna—we should not be the ones to tie the noose of definition around the Christ—the "Man for Others" —who entered the world—becoming the first and last "Human Being," which is the way the phrase Son of Man should be translated. We who gather here today have come to know God in the face of Christ. We thank God for that face first glimpsed by the world in the child of Bethlehem. We should not let our small and petty restrictions and constrictions to limit the destiny of this One as the liberator, fulfiller, and eternal homebringer of all human beings who have ever been or will ever be earth people. As for the other billions of habitable planets in these galaxies—we'll leave that to God and C. S. Lewis.

As I finish this sermon here in Cambridge, I wonder as I wander whether Jesus was so much a human that he had brothers like James and sisters, and I ask whether mother Miriam was just a *Jungfrau*—a human young girl as Luther seemed to believe, or whether she was the immaculately conceived Virgin—the gate-keeper of heaven. A white beard theologian-pastor should know those things by now. I have just heard a splendid lecture on St. Augustine and his doctrine of omnipresence. The professor is from Bordeaux. Having just greeted Advent last night and meditating on the incarnation, I close with two phrases from the Bishop of Hippo on the meaning of the mystery of the Incarnation:

> God is not absent even from the one in whom it is thought He does not dwell.

> He comes without being who he was, Presence, whether or not we greet him—he always comes everywhere and anywhere—ever anew.

TRUE HUMAN and VERY GOD OF VERY GOD.

# 19

# True God[1]

THE DEEP MYSTERY OF the Advent, Christmas, and Epiphany season comes to rest in the lectionary today from the Gospel of John: "The Word was made flesh"—there's that irascibly human thing again—it continues—"and dwelt"—literally pitched his tent—among us—but now something new is added—"full of Grace and Truth"—a cowstall—full of Glory—incredible! I love the way that Gian Carlo Menotti puts it in the opera *Amahl and the Night Visitors*—which narrates last week's Matthew text. Melchior the king, with his two magi fellow searchers for the child, sings it with Amahl's mother—"Have you seen a child the color of earth, the color of thorn, his hands are those of the poor as poor he was born?"—Earth child for sure—then more: "Have you seen a child—the color of wheat the color of dawn—his hands are those of a king as King he was born?" This is something new.

Sara and I sang and played this work in the little town of Watseka, Illinois, where we were pastors—fifty years ago. We also slipped down to the little town movie theater to see the just-released Italian film: Pier Paolo Passolini's *Gospel According to St. Matthew*. This was as "down to earth" a film that you will find—as we did—full of beauty and radiance—as a little Italian mountain village with its poor workers become the actors of Matthew's narrative.

Today's text is "The color of wheat the color of dawn," even though "earth and thorn" hover near. John's Gospel is so otherworldly we wonder

1. January 5, 2014. Text: John 1.

if John has ever heard the Bethlehem story or even the earth story of Jesus. The whole Gospel seems to be about Jesus' last seventy-two hours and about the theological mystery of who he is. Yet—we are quite confident that he knew Jesus—he was with him all along, but he focused his memory—written many decades later, especially on his death and resurrection, his ascension and promised return. He is serene and victorious—even more than Paul—Earth has become wheat—thorn has become dawn.

Of this John text, Raymond Brown has said in his book *The Birth of the Messiah* that if the synoptic Gospels are about the sayings and gospel of Jesus/Messiah, then John is about the Messiah's signs and glory. Both treatments are authentic works of the disciples Matthew and the young John who reclined on the heart of his master; think of Da Vinci's *Last Supper* or Dali's.

Here is the "Message of John" according to the insights of Raymond Brown. After Paul and perhaps with greater wisdom than the late-born apostle—John becomes the author of the theological and anthropological system of the early church. John's book is the truth about God and man.

Here's how it goes: The Word is made flesh (1:14); Human wrong has placed flesh and matter under what John calls "the power of Satan" (I John 5:19); Jesus conquered this misrule (21:31); Now the common elements of bread, water, and wine have become Jesus flesh and blood tokens—taking on power over the world, flesh, devil and death—the array of enemies of God. Since this is a moral Jewish text and not a mystical Greek text, the glory of God renders human sinful flesh quiescent and powerless as the salvation of Christ remakes us into the kingdom of God where water, bread, light, and life become life foods for us. Brown anchors this interpretation in the evidence of Qumran, where John the Baptist, perhaps even Jesus himself, are implicated in what those texts address as the "Teacher of Righteousness"—a redeeming Messiah—for whom the world has long waited—has come.

TRUE GOD is the way that the Scripture and creed would say this. One has now appeared at the back door of the world and at the front doors of our hearts—to bring this about for all space, time, and creation. Indeed, this is what creation, incarnation and new creation is. What are the practical working out of these truths in our everyday lives?

First, if there is one truth, there is one God and no other. We saw a new film recently in Cambridge with my son Bert, a professor there, and his with-child partner—Leonie—a Scottish lassie. The film was *Hunger Games*:

## True God

*Catching Fire*, starring Jennifer Lawrence. The story is about a futuristic technological state where all people are subjected in terror by a few leaders of wealth and power who control the entire populace of thirteen districts with a robotic army, surveillance and media announcers of the genre of "survival" TV programs. The god of this Brave New World is surrendered freedom and total domination of all people. But there is a primitive underside to this great public machine. In the jungles, mountains, and seashores, a small band of revolutionary free spirits defy the corrupt system and with bravery, love for others and acts of truth and mercy—even sacrifice (greater love). With these anti-system virtues, they overcome the tyranny's terror and, person by person, district by district—bring back a free and humane society. God and Truth is now the sole authority.

TRUE GOD tolerates no false gods or god substitute idols—things like money, power, nations, violence. Liberty and democracy is fashioned and sustained in such iconoclastic realms. Today much of the world—even the West and our own nation—offspring of belief in the ONE TRUE GOD—are becoming security states, belligerent states, places where wealth is craved at the expense of the poor and common people—the sick, homeless, less-privileged, young and old, immigrants, persons of different lifestyles and values. This nation, speaking of Herod, has become a state where torture (Guantanamo), even infanticide (Cleveland) are not unknown. Such disdain and downright harm is unacceptable in a TRUE GOD world. We either serve "The God who failed" or the TRUE GOD. There is no other choice. It is either "Darkness at Noon" or "The Light that shines in the darkness and the darkness cannot put it out" (John 1:5).

John 3:16 is the whole Gospel in miniature. "God loved the world so—the *cosmos*—the whole fallen system—all that world was meant to be and what we have made of it. That he gave his only begotten and beloved son." I've been preaching this text to you for twenty years—It is the heart of all that I believe and have to say, and you are people of my heart. *Monogenos*—the only one—begotten—not made— says Nicea—I can't get my head around that—*Agapetos*—now that I can comprehend and live and die for—his beloved child. That whoever believes in him should not perish but have eternal life. That's enough for me. That is the whole meaning of the beginning and the end— the creation of creation and the end of the creation—Christmas and Easter. TRUE GOD of TRUE GOD—VERY GOD of VERY GOD. Those bishops who limped to Nicea—their Achilles tendons had been slashed—or they were led—for they had been blinded by their persecutors—when they came to put their message into words they ran out of superlatives.

So that's about it. True man and True God: two sermons. Go now with grace into the future of this One God—Father, Son and Spirit—and that peace and hope, love and joy—go with you! AMEN.[2]

---

2. Comment: This concluding set of sermons is "Vintage Vaux"—it having just been offered one year ago. The reader will see continuities and innovations between what has gone before. One finds here not *reductio ad absurdum* but *reductio ad theologium*—every matter is seen as ultimately a theological matter. If I had been a teacher in the secular university rather than the seminary, I might well have become a more empirical and analytical thinker. But my habits have made me a restless exponent of the view that we humans are *homo religiosis*.

# Conclusion and Appraisal

I ADMIT TO BEING a creature of nostalgia. I was brought up to believe in great preaching and great preachers. The greatest preachers of all time were St. Augustine, Paul, Jesus, and Moses. Others of particular note were Francis of Assisi, Thomas of Aquino, Martin Luther of Wittenberg, and John Calvin of Geneva, Karl Barth of Basel, and Reinhold Niebuhr of Detroit, Toyohiko Kagawa of Tokyo, Dietrich Bonhoeffer of Berlin, and Martin Luther King, Jr. of Atlanta.

Numerous parents, grandparents and other solicitors thought that I was, was born to be, or was meant to be, or should have been, a great preacher. My paternal grandmother, mother, and mother-in-law all knew I was meant for greatness. My grandfathers and father, father-in-law, sons and daughters, friends and neighbors, were more sanguine or skeptical.

I was blessed by being the student of persons who were thought to be the great preachers of the modern age: George Buttrick and Paul Scherer of Princeton Seminary, James Stewart of Edinburgh, and Helmut Thielicke of Hamburg. In recent years. I have been positively transformed by the likes of John Buchanan of Chicago, and Calum MacLeod of Chicago, now Edinburgh (St. Giles).

I'm not at all sure as I reach my seventy-fifth year of age and fiftieth year as a preacher whether the above was a concocted myth, a desperate hope, or in some way—partially true and valid.

That I have bound these nineteen sermons into one folio—nineteen of perhaps 190 down in a rusty file cabinet in the basement—evidences some fantasy—even audacity. Perhaps my dear wife of fifty years, Sara, who stoked the illusion that I had something worth the saying and worth the hearing, is behind it all.

## Second Sermons

The reader and the dear friends who came out at three parishes and countless one-shot-stand-ins will be the ultimate judges, and even more the One, whom Schweitzer—not a bad preacher himself—still found at the lakeside beaconing—"Follow Me."

Kenneth Vaux—November 30, 2014

# Bibliography

Bancroft, Richard. *Sermon on Christ, Government and the Church*. Bancroft papers at Pusey House, Oxford. 1600.
Barth, Karl. *Church Dogmatics*. Vol. III/3. Edinburgh: T. & T. Clark, 1952.
———. *Dogmatics in Outline*. New York: Harper, 1959.
Bonhoeffer, Dietrich. *The Cost of Discipleship*. Translated by R. H. Fuller. New York: Simon & Schuster, 1959.
———. *Ethics*. Translated by Reinhard Krauss, Charles C. West, and Douglas W. Stott. Philadelphia: Fortress, 2004.
———. *No Rusty Swords: Letters, Lectures and Notes, 1928–1936*. Edited by Edwin H. Robertson. Translated by Edwin H. Robertson and John Bowden. New York: Harper & Row, 1965.
Brown, Raymond. T*he Birth of the Messiah: A Commentary on the Infancy Narratives in the Gospels of Matthew and Luke*. New Haven, CT: Yale University Press, 1999.
Bunyan, John. *The Pilgrim's Progress*. London: C. Brightly and T. Einnersley, 1809.
Calvin, John. *Commentary on 2 Corinthians*. Library of Christian Classics. Philadelphia, Westminster, 1964.
Cicero. *Tusculan Disputations*. Loeb Classical Library. Cambridge, MA: Harvard University Press, 1927.
Erikson, Erik. *Gandhi's Truth: On the Origins of Militant Non-Violence*. New York: Norton, 1969.
Fischer, Louis. *The Life of Mahatma Gandhi*. New York: Harper, 1958.
Frost, Robert. *In the Clearing*. New York: Henry Holt, 1995.
Gandhi, Mahatma. *Satyagraha*. Delhi, 1950.
Garside, Charles. *Zwingli and the Arts*. New Haven, CT: Yale University Press, 1966.
Herbert, George. "Let All the World in Every Corner Sing." London, 1633.
Hordern, William. *A Layman's Guide to Protestant Theology*. Eugene, OR: Wipf & Stock, 2002.
Hugo, Victor. *Les Miserables*. New York: Signet, 2014.
*Jewish Prayer Book*. Authorized Version. New York: Block, 1948.
Jonas, Hans. "The Burden and Blessing of Mortality." *The Hastings Center Report* 22/1 (March 23, 1992) 34–40.
Jones, E. Stanley. *Mahatma Gandhi*. London: Hodder and Stoughton, 1948.

## BIBLIOGRAPHY

Kevles, Daniel. *In the Name of Eugenics.* Cambridge, MA: Harvard University Press, 1998.
Lewis, C. S. *The Horse and His Boy,* New York: Harper & Row, 1954.
———. *The Lion, the Witch and the Wardrobe,* New York: Harper & Row, 1950.
———. *The Last Battle,* New York: Harper & Row, 1956.
———. *The Magician's Nephew,* New York: Harper & Row, 1955.
———. *Mere Christianity.* New York: Simon & Schuster, 1971.
———. *Prince Caspian,* New York: Harper & Row, 1951.
———. *The Silver Chair,* New York: Harper & Row, 1953.
———. *The Voyage of the Dawn Treader,* New York: Harper & Row, 1952.
Marcuse, Herbert. *One-Dimensional Man: Studies in the Ideology of Advanced Industrial Society.* Boston: Beacon, 1964.
Meeks, Wayne. *The Moral World of the First Christians.* Philadelphia: Westminster, 1986.
Menotti, Gian-Carlo. *Amahl and the Night Visitors.* Opera commissioned by NBC, December 24, 1951.
Moltmann, Jurgen. *Theology of Hope.* Translated by James W. Leitch. London: SCM, 1967.
Outler, Albert. *Evangelism and Theology in the Wesleyan Spirit.* Nashville: Abingdon, 2000.
Rilke, Rainer Maria. *Rilke's Book of Hours: Love Poems to God.* Translated by Joanna Macy and Anita Barrows. London: Penguin, 1997.
Sandburg, Carl. *Abraham Lincoln: A Biography.* New York: Harcourt & Brace, 1926.
Sandel, Michael. *The Case Against Perfection.* Cambridge, MA: Harvard University Press, 2007.
Schweitzer, Albert. *J. S. Bach.* Vol. 1. Translated by Ernest Newman. New York: Dover, 1966.
Shaffer, Peter. *Amadeus: A Play.* New York: Harper Perennial, 2001.
Stringfellow, William. *A Public and Private Faith.* Grand Rapids: Eerdmans, 1962.
Teilhard de Chardin, Pierre. *On Suffering.* NewYork: Harper & Row, 2001.
Tendulkar, Mahesh. *Mahatma.* Vol 1. New Delhi: Publications of India, 1950.
Tillich, Paul. *The Courage to Be.* New Haven, CT: Yale University Press, 1952.
Vaux, Kenneth. "Debbie's Dying." *JAMA* 259/14 (April 1988) 2140–41.
———. *The Ministry of Vincent Van Gogh in Religion and Art.* Eugene, OR: Wipf & Stock, 2012.
Wink, Walter. *The Human Being: Jesus and the Enigma of the Son of Man.* Philadelphia: Fortress, 2001.
Wordsworth, William. "Ode: Intimations of Immortality from Recollections of Early Childhood." http://www.poetryfoundation.org/poem/174805.

www.ingramcontent.com/pod-product-compliance
Lightning Source LLC
Chambersburg PA
CBHW071506150426
43191CB00009B/1435